Successful Hunting Strategies

Successful Hunting Strategies

Hunter's Information Series ®
North American Hunting Club
Minneapolis, Minnesota

Successful Hunting Strategies

Library of Congress Catalog Card Number 92-60740
ISBN 0-914697-49-8

Printed in U.S.A.
   3   4   5   6   7   8   9

The North American Hunting Club
offers a line of hats for hunters.
For information, write:
     North American Hunting Club
     P.O. Box 3401
     Minneapolis, MN 55343

Contents

Acknowledgments

The North American Hunting Club would like to thank everyone who helped create this book.

Artist David Rottinghaus provided all illustrations. Photos were provided by Bear Archery, Cabela's, Paul DeMarchi, *North American Hunter* Senior Editor Dan Dietrich, Tom Edwards, Farm Form Inc., Bob Hagel, David Hofius, Mark Kayser, *North American Hunter* Publisher Mark LaBarbera, *North American Hunter* Editor Bill Miller, Neal and Mary Jane Mishler, Steve Pennaz, Remington, Leonard Lee Rue III, Leonard Lee Rue IV, Nick Sisley, Richard P. Smith, Hal Swiggett, Irene Vandermolen, Chris Van Eimeren and Bill Vaznis. The cover photo was provided by Charles J. Alsheimer.

A special thanks to the North American Hunting Club's publications staff for all their efforts: Publisher Mark LaBarbera, Editor Bill Miller, Managing Editor of Books Ron Larsen, Associate Editor of Books Colleen Ferguson and Editorial Assistant Mary Petrie-Terry. Thanks also to Vice President of Product Marketing Mike Vail, Marketing Manager Cal Franklin and Marketing Project Coordinator Laura Resnik.

Foreword

Excitement. Adventure. The best hunting strategies from North America's finest outdoor writers. Those are the elements that the North American Hunting Club staff has skillfully combined to create *Successful Hunting Strategies*. You won't find a book quite like it anywhere else.

As you peruse the pages of this edition, you'll be stunned by the depth of coverage on all aspects of hunting. Instead of a single expert's opinion on varied hunting topics, presented here are the views of more than a dozen great outdoorsmen, each writing on his area of greatest expertise. You might say this work is the best from the best.

Along with the inside look at successful hunting strategies for deer, bear, mountain game, waterfowl, upland birds and more, this book offers excitement and adventure—the real reasons we all hunt. *Successful Hunting Strategies* will be referenced again and again for enhancement of hunting skills and to relive heart-stopping moments afield.

For example, you'll share the most exciting adventures of hunting legends like Fred Bear. In this title, the NAHC has been granted permission to publish the photo series of Fred's successful bowhunt for Alaskan brown bear. While the quality of reproduction may suffer, these photos are among the most unique hunting images ever acquired and are certainly worthy of publication. This

"hunting video" of yesteryear is historical documentation of Fred Bear's prowess as a hunter and an archer. And it is just plain exciting.

Elsewhere in the book, you'll get down to brass tacks on whitetail hunting strategies with renowned hunter and writer Hal Swiggett. *North American Hunter* editor Bill Miller shares his favorite waterfowl decoying strategies and a new approach for hunting pheasants. Lloyd Bare takes you to the top of the continent in search of trophy rams and billies. Bob Hagel presents straightforward handloading tips for the hunter. Richard Smith helps you follow the trail of a wounded black bear. And that's only a sampling of what *Successful Hunting Strategies* has to offer.

In preparing this title, the NAHC staff considered the most commonly asked questions from NAHC Members. They then sought to pull together the advice of the experts to answer those questions. Those answers and more comprise this book.

For your money, you probably won't be able to find a better, more complete hunting title anywhere, at least with so much sound advice from such a wide array of experienced hunters and communicators. In its pages you'll probably confirm a lot of your own thoughts on your favorite kind of hunting and learn some new things about types of hunting you want to learn more about. Either way, *Successful Hunting Strategies* certainly will have accomplished its goal.

Enjoy this Hunter's Information Series book and all of your time in the woods.

Steven F. Burke
President
North American Hunting Club

1

Handgunning For Whitetails

by Hal Swiggett

The subject of handgun hunting for white-tailed deer covers a lot of ground, literally.

Some of us hunt where 75 to 100 yards would be as close a shot as we're ever likely to get. Others of us hunt where 50 yards would be a *l-o-o-n-g* shot.

Some hunt from tree stands shooting at animals that are totally unaware of a human in the area. Often these shots are from 10 or 15 yards to a maximum of 25 or 30. Hunting from blinds on the ground usually allows shots at no more than 35 to 50 yards.

Revolvers For Deer Hunting

Tree-stand hunters can get away with .357 Rem. Mag. handguns if they are careful shooters. The animals are unaware of trouble and are a lot easier to drop in their tracks with the lesser bullet weight and, therefore, energy of .357 Rem. Mag. cartridge.

Those hunting from ground blinds can, again if they are cautious and careful hunters, tag their buck with the .357 Rem. Mag. Shots do have to be kept to 50 yards at the maximum and perfectly placed to assure venison for the freezer.

I know, I sound back-offish from the .357 Rem. Mag. You would too if you had seen as many deer killed as I have. And trailed as many. And lost as many because of blood trails fading, resulting from incomplete bullet penetration. Good blood trails come from

Hal Swiggett has been shooting handguns for over 60 years. Here he tests a Remington XP-100 at a range session for outdoor media.

exit holes, not from bullet entrance wounds.

If you're still set on using a .357 Rem. Mag. for hunting deer-sized critters at least use a cartridge packing a 180-grain bullet. Don't even consider anything less than 158 grains unless you can, literally, be right on top of a deer—and a small one at that!

As for handloading, I've been told (by shooters who should know) that 14 grains of H110 under the 180-grain bullet does a fine job in the .357 Mag. and that six more grains in the .357 Maximum does even better. I still say that a properly loaded .44 Rem. Mag is so superior to the .357s that the .357 isn't even worth considering for hunting.

Shooters of the Colt .45—often, but incorrectly, referred to as .45 Long Colt—can do little better than stuff 10 grains of Unique under a hard-cast 250- or 260-grain Keith-style bullet.

I have shot hundreds of these through a .45 Colt Abilene 6-inch single action. This combination took 28 deer-sized exotics in three days during a culling operation on a very large ranch. No shot was more than 60 yards and no animal ran more than 60 yards. All but one was shot through the lungs.

That one animal took a step as I dropped the hammer. My bullet hit "too far back." (Maybe you have noticed: Gun writers

White-tailed bucks rub small trees to remove velvet from their antlers. If a handgunner hunts near sign like this, he can expect a shot within range of a wheelgun.

never make a gut shot—it's always a little "too far back.") A fast second shot went where it was supposed to. The others were all one-shot kills.

For those shots beyond 50 yards, the .44 Rem. Mag. should really be considered minimum for the wheelgun hunter. Factory 240-grain loads are more or less effective at 50 to 60 yards; but, do not depend upon them beyond that.

Federal has some good .44 Rem. Mag. loads if you insist on hunting with factory fodder. Winchester Silvertip bullets, on the other hand, are not good for big-game handgun hunting. They expand too rapidly and provide insufficient penetration for deer-sized or larger game. However, I must emphatically point out that, in this case, I'm strictly talking about handgunning with the .44 Rem. Mag! Silvetips designed for and loaded in rifle cartridges are superb for big-game hunting!

Most experienced handgun hunters use bullets heavier than 240 grains in the .44 Rem. Mag. This means handloading.

Hornady offers a good 265-grain jacketed bullet. Sierra has a new 300-grain jacketed soft point that is a beauty. Until Sierra brought out this new 300-grain JSP I was a confirmed 320-grain cast bullet shooter.

I have used J.D.'s 320-grain cast bullets extensively, both in this country and in Africa, and finally got one back out of an animal a couple of years ago. My first shot went, as directed, through the top of a 5x5 bull's heart. He turned and ran straight away. A second shot went in just to the right of his tail, scraped along the backbone, and was retrieved from under the hide in front of his left shoulder.

Full length through a mature bull elk! Outstanding penetration such as this does not come from light or expanding bullets. And, in my estimation, it does take deep penetration to kill big game quickly and cleanly.

For the .44 Rem. Mag. most loading manuals will take you through 240 to 265-grain bullets, but only Hodgdon's Data Manual goes on to 300-grain. I am always hesitant about quoting loads because I have no control over your loading bench. My Ruger .44 Mag. guns, both Super Redhawk and Super Blackhawk, comfortably digest 21.5 grains of H110 or W296 under 320-grain, hardcast bullets. It was with this load that my bullet went full length through the elk.

This load is only for Ruger guns, and only after you've sort of sneaked up on it. Do not try to shoot this load in a fine Model 29 Smith & Wesson. They are built for factory ammunition only. Not heavy handloads. If you shoot your Model 29 with factory ammunition, or equivalent handloads, and keep your shots to 50 or 60 yards with 75 as tops when positive of a good hit, you will have no trouble.

Many handgun hunters are moving up to the .454 Casull, myself included, though I will never commit my Ruger .44s to retirement.

The .454 Casull, designed 30-plus years ago by Dick Casull, has made it to the top as a hunter's repeating handgun. Nothing even comes close to it!

But only, and I can't emphasize this enough, for the experienced handgunner! When the .454 Casull is loaded to maximum power for hunting, recoil is beyond controllability for the beginning or occasional shooter. This gun is an effective, sophisticated tool for the experienced handgunner.

Deep penetration is needed to kill big game quickly and cleanly. Be careful when choosing loads for your handgun. Some models can only handle factory ammunition.

The .454 Casull is one of the most popular handguns for big-game hunters. Because of its recoil when loaded to maximum power, this cartridge is for experienced handgunners—not beginners.

Obviously, the .454 Casull can be loaded down; however, if that is going to be done there is no point in spending the extra dollars; all you'll have is a glorified .44 Rem. Mag. in an expensive gun. To learn to shoot a Casull, use a heavily loaded .44 Mag. until experienced enough to handle the bigger gun.

Single-Shot Pistols

Moving on to longer distances demands the use of rifle or rifle-like cartridges. This means Thompson/Center, Pachmayr Dominator, Remington XP-100 or one of the custom bolt-action pistols.

Thompson/Center's best for deer hunting is their "Super 14" barrel in either .30-30 Win. or .35 Rem. I have used both extensively. In fact, I used a T/C 14-inch to prove the accuracy of Winchester's new Supreme .30-30 cartridge when it first hit dealer's shelves. It consistently shot less than 1-inch, 3-shot groups at 100 yards.

When shooting factory loads in a .30-30 Win., it's best to use

When shooting from longer distances, the Thomson/Center Contender in 30-30 Win. is extremely accurate. Hal recommends 150-grain bullets with this caliber.

150-grain loads. (Even 125s work well from a pistol-length barrel.) Even though these have lighter jackets, some velocity is lost through the shorter-than-rifle-length barrel, which prevents them from doing their work well.

Factory 150-grain .35 Rem. ammunition does a rather good job in either the T/C or XP-100 chambered for this round. Handloaders can increase the velocity considerably in the XP, over factory .35 Rem. ammunition. Why? Because factory ammunition has to be usable in older lever guns. My XP .35 Rem. 200-grain loads run close to 500 fps over factory velocity for rifles.

Remington over-the-counter XP-100 pistols, for deer hunters are either 7mm BR Rem. or .35 Rem. For the so-inclined shooter, 7mm BR XPs can easily be rechambered by a skilled gunsmith for the great 7mm-08 Rem. rifle cartridge. This chambering is also available directly from Remington's Custom Shop, but the price is considerably higher than the rechambered, garden-variety XP that I shoot.

Pachmayr's Dominator single shot is offered in .44 Mag. or 7mm-08 Rem. I shoot one of the latter a lot. It was set up for me to use in Pachmayr's video, "Handgun Hunting With Hal Swiggett," and has even made a trip to South Africa.

Rifle cartridges in handguns can effectively stretch reliable killing distances out to 150 to 250 yards, depending upon the shooter's ability and the cartridge selected.

Moving on up the ladder in single-shot hunting handguns we reach the top rung with J.D. Jones and his SSK Custom barrels. By far the most popular is his .375 JDJ, which is a full-length .444 Marlin case necked down to accept .375 bullets. I've used one a lot, both here and in Africa. It will start 270-grain bullets at close to 2,000 feet per second.

Good hunters will have no trouble getting their venison with handguns. In fact, good hunters seldom have to shoot at a deer beyond 100 yards; blind and tree-stand hunters are even closer.

A Great Track Record

They say the proof is in the pudding, so without bragging, let's take a look at 10 handgun whitetail kills I've been part of on recent hunts. These should convince you that handguns are indeed adequate medicine for whitetail hunting.

Number 10: He dropped in his tracks from a 270-grain Hornady .375 JDJ bullet through the neck. Propelled by 44.9 grains of H322, the bullet left the muzzle of the .375 JDJ/SSK Thompson/

Rifle cartridges in handguns can take trophy whitetails out to traditional rifle distances. NAHC Editor Bill Miller proved it with his T/C Contender in .30-30 Win.

Center (T/C) barrel at close to 2,000 feet per second (fps).

Number 9: She dropped in her tracks from a 300-grain Sierra .4295 bullet through the neck. Propelled by 30.5 grains of H296, the bullet left the muzzle of the Dan Wesson .445 Super Mag. at about 1,300 fps.

Number 8: He didn't drop in his tracks because the shot was flubbed. The second 300-grain Sierra .4295 bullet, same load and gun as in Number 9, put the period to my error.

Number 7: He dropped in his tracks from a 200-grain Hornady .358 bullet through the neck. Propelled by H4198, this bullet exited the muzzle of the XP-100 Remington .35 Rem. at close to 2,300 fps.

Number 6: He ran about 40 yards before dropping from a Remington 140-grain, 7mm-08 factory load through the lungs. The bullet was fired from a Pachmayr Dominator.

Number 5: The buck dropped 55 steps from where the 320-grain, hard-cast JDJ bullet went through his lungs. Propelled by 21.5 grains of W296, the bullet was fired from a Mag-Na-Ported Stalker (8⅜-inch custom Ruger Super Blackhawk) and left the muzzle at about 1,300 fps.

Number 4: He fell where he was hit with the 300-grain Freedom Arms bullet going through both shoulders. It left the muzzle of the 7½-inch .454 Casull at close to 1,800 fps, kicked out by 31.5 grains of H110.

Number 3: She dropped 37 steps from where the above bullet/handgun combination drove the bullet through the heart.

Number 2: He fell where he was standing when the Remington 240-grain jacketed soft point (factory load) went through the neck, a few inches in front of the shoulders. It was fired from a customized Ruger Super Blackhawk with a 4⅝-inch barrel.

Number 1: He ran close to 60 yards after being hit with a 240-grain hard-cast lead bullet, which was started on its way by 23.5 grains of H110 and fired from the same Ruger Super Blackhawk as in Number 2.

These are all white-tailed deer and were killed in the order listed, Number 10 being the most recent. There were 40 to 50 deer-sized and considerably larger animals killed in this same time frame, but whitetails are the subject here.

Number 10, a young 8-pointer, was shot at about 40 yards. He was rattled up. This is the reason for the long-range pistol: I was hunting in deep South Texas and had prepared for a long shot at a big deer. The opportunity never came. With the 4X Bausch &

A good shooting glove is recommended when big-bore handgunning. It provides added comfort from the recoil that is common with heavy loads.

Lomb scope, he could have just as easily been dropped at about 200 yards.

Numbers 9 and 8 were taken while researching the new Dan Wesson .445 Super Mag. It is a .44 Mag. in case diameter, but ballistically I'm still out on it. The revolver is built for .44 Mag. pressure but the case length doesn't fit those specifications. Let's wait this one out. Light bullets, 180 to 240 grains, can achieve sufficiently more velocity over the conventional .44 Mag.; however, heavy hunting bullets are still questionable in my mind.

Number 7 was a prime 9-pointer (started as a 10 but one tine broke off during a fight). This load is safe in my XP-100 Remington bolt action pistol, but you are on your own if you try it. Do not try this in a T/C or any of the old lever-action rifles. It produces a little over 500 fps more velocity, out of the 14-inch XP, than Remington factory loads. The shot was at 90 to 100 yards and the buck was walking into some thick cover.

Number 6 was shot a little over 100 yards, probably closer to 125. The Dominator Conversion Unit is permanently attached to the .45 autoloader frame and the trigger adjusted down to 1½ pounds. There is a 3X Pachmayr scope on top. If using one of these conversion units on a Colt-type frame that you intend to convert back to a semi-auto, do not lighten the trigger. A slide on mine would probably be a dangerous problem.

Number 5 was shot at 86 steps—69 or 70 yards. My steps average 29 inches, so I multiply that by the number taken then divide by 36 (inches in a yard). I think I am mighty close to correct.

The customized Ruger wears a 2X Leupold scope and has killed game in several states and in Africa. It was used, with the same load, in a video done for the Jicarilla Apache Indian Tribe. The 5x5 bull elk is shown as he comes to the bugle. I hit him in the heart, then again as he spun around and departed. I could see, as I fired the second shot, he was going down but let go anyway to be safe. The tape, soon to be released, is titled "Hunting the Jicarilla High Country With Hal Swiggett."

Numbers 4 and 3 were taken on the same hunt. The buck in Number 4 was shot at 121 steps, close to 91 or 92 yards. My 7½-inch .454 Casull is topped with a 2X Leupold. The load came from Dick Casull's mouth to my ear via telephone. He suggested 30 to 33 grains of H110. I split the difference, used 31.5, and have found no reason to change. The five-shooter recoils enough with the 1.5 grains less than his full charge. Dead is dead, and that is what has happened every time one of the 300-grain jacketed Freedom Arms flat-nosed bullets has hit flesh and bone. This is in the 1,700 to 1,800 fps velocity range.

The doe in Number 3 was hit through the top of the heart at 153 steps (123 to 124 yards). Admittedly not intentional. I was aiming for the center of the lungs some four or so inches higher. No handgunner in his right mind (in my opinion) would try a heart shot at that distance. One needs only to remember a bullet lower than the heart is either a miss (if lucky) or a broken leg.

Numbers 2 and 1 were taken with the same customized .44 Mag. Ruger Super Blackhawk. The barrel was shortened to 4⅝ inches, Mag-Na-Ported and fitted with a brass bead up front and a shallow "V" in back. This same customizing method is used for African dangerous game by professional hunters on their fast-action rifles for backing up clients.

I'm sure I wasn't the first, but would have to be among that group to try this sight on a revolver. Ruger later came out with a

Hal Swiggett has shot many white-tailed deer with various handguns. This is a Texas buck Hal took in his home state.

similar arrangement for their interchangeable sighted double-action Redhawk. Freedom Arms also lists it as an option on the fine Casull single actions. My .454, 4⅝-inch is so rigged. This is a very fast and surprisingly accurate sighting system.

Both of these bucks were killed on the same hunt, Number 2 with Remington's 240 JSP factory load and Number 1 with my long-preferred handload. I had hoped to see the difference in performance between a hard-cast, Keith-type 240 and 23.5 grains of H110 and the factory offering. I learned absolutely nothing.

Number 1 ran about 60 yards with the bullet through the center of its lungs. Number 2 was shot in the neck. Neither bullet was recovered. The lung-shot buck was at 63 steps (close to 50 yards) and the neck-shot at 46 steps (37 yards). For the 37-yard shot I worked my way into a brisk breeze and through a live oak thicket. The buck jumped up out of his bed, looked around a tree to see what was there and dropped in his tracks. All I could see was his head and neck.

I hope I have helped relieve you of doubt and reservations concerning the ability of handguns to take deer-sized game. I've been hunting with them for more than 60 years and have yet to see reason to give it up!

2

Trailing And Field Dressing

by Dan Dietrich

Sometimes every piece of the hunting puzzle fits perfectly into place. Scouting, practice and stand selection all come together, and you execute a perfect shot. When this happens the result should be a well-deserved smile for the camera and a freezer full of tasty meat. However, one important step has yet to be taken.

Following a blood trail requires common sense, patience and attention to detail. It is not rocket science. But how well you follow up your shot determines whether, at day's end, you will experience success or frustration. And once you've found your game, how you field dress the animal determines the flavor and quality of the meat. This chapter will show you straightforward strategies to trail and recover big-game animals. It will also take you step-by-step through the field-dressing and caping process.

All modern hunting tackle is capable of cleanly and efficiently harvesting every big game animal in North America. As well-known bowhunter Chuck Adams wrote in *North American Hunter*, "No animal in North America can survive a broadhead through both lungs." Nor can one survive a bullet through both lungs. Chuck, of course, is the first bowhunter in history to harvest North America's 27 recognized big-game species.

While the end result is the same—a cleanly taken game animal—there is a significant difference between how a firearm and a bow achieve the end result. A modern firearm has the potential to kill a big-game animal by concussion (i.e., a bullet or slug delivers sufficient foot-pounds of kinetic energy to instantaneously kill the animal). A mule deer I shot in Wyoming with a rifle, for example, went down before I recovered from the shot's recoil. This doesn't happen every time, but we have all heard similar accounts. If a bullet does not kill by concussion, it must then harvest the game animal through hemorrhaging.

A bow and arrow is designed to efficiently harvest game animals through hemorrhaging. A razor-sharp broadhead delivered to the heart or lungs of a big-game animal will often dispatch that animal in less than 60 seconds. That's not much time. However, during those few seconds, a startled animal can easily cover more than 100 yards. On other shots it will take much longer. Gut-shot animals may take several hours to expire.

All hunters who do not drop the animal with the first shot will have to use their blood trailing and game recovery skills. No matter how open the terrain or how good the first shot, never assume you will be able to simply walk to the spot where you last saw or heard the animal and recover your game. Many hunters would be ecstatic if game recovery were that easy.

Successful Trailing Strategies

Successful trailing begins the moment you pull the trigger or release the arrow. As you shoot, keep your concentration on the aiming point. In addition to this being proper shooting form, bowhunters might catch a glimpse of their arrow as it penetrates the game. Also listen for the sound of your hit. Gun hunters will sometimes hear the bullet penetrate game. And bowhunters will often hear a quick punch as the arrow penetrates. A soggy, slushy-sounding hit often indicates a complete pass through; an abbreviated, solid punch often indicates the arrow encountered bone. Whether or not you see or hear the result of your shot, watch for a reaction from the animal.

Sometimes a fatally hit game animal will bolt a short distance, then stop and look over its shoulder to where it was standing. Stay completely quiet. Watch the animal closely. If you can place another shot in the vitals, do it. Note any tree and/or shrub it passes. Watch how it runs or walks until you can no longer see it. Then listen for its progress until you can no longer hear it.

When you can no longer see or hear the game, mentally map out what happened and determine the direction the animal was traveling. If you have a compass, take a reading of the direction it

Trailing and recovering your big-game animal requires persistence and common sense. Follow the strategies set forth in this chapter and your trailing efforts should result in a well-deserved smile.

was heading. Next, note the exact spot the animal was standing when you shot. Pick out trees, shrubs or landmarks—as many as you can—which the animal passed. If you have a map of the area or a piece of paper, quietly sketch out what happened. Put an ''X'' in the spot the animal was standing. Draw the route it traveled and note those landmarks it ran past. Write down the compass bearing. And make a brief note about how the animal reacted to your shot.

While fatally hit animals never react exactly the same, there are typical reactions. A well-hit big-game animal, for instance, usually runs with its tail down. A heart-shot animal may instantly charge off, showing no sign of being hit. A gut-shot animal will often hunch its back when hit.

What you do after the shot depends on the weather, time of day, hunting conditions, hunting tool and shot placement.

Weather and time of day will influence your decision on when to start blood trailing game. Given ideal conditions—no rain and more than one hour of remaining daylight—gun hunters and bowhunters should sit for at least 30 minutes (preferably one hour) after the shot. Why? Because often a well-hit animal will travel a short distance, then bed down. If you start following the animal too soon after the shot or start making excessive noise you could keep the animal on the move. And the farther the animal travels, the more difficult it is to find it.

Less than ideal hunting conditions may force you to begin blood trailing earlier, and in so doing, risk the chance of pushing your game. For example, rain or snow can quickly wash away or cover up a blood trail. Waiting 30 minutes to an hour under these conditions could leave you with little if any blood sign so that trailing is impossible. Instead, under these conditions, use the point of impact as the starting point and determine the animal's direction and speed of travel.

Time of day must also be considered. If you shoot an animal just before the closing of legal shooting hours, find the blood trail as quickly as possible that evening rather than hoping you can pick it up the next morning. Rain or snow could fall during the night, and unless you have marked the point of impact and at least started to follow the blood trail to determine the direction of travel, your chances of recovering your game will be greatly reduced.

On hunts where you are not familiar with the terrain, exercise caution before you start traipsing through the country looking for blood sign; this is especially true out West in the rugged and remote areas. A lost hunter—anywhere in North America—will hinder rather than help the game recovery effort. On guided big-game hunts, guides will often request that a hunter wait for assistance before starting to trail or follow game. The guide most likely is familiar with the area and probably knows the most likely route of travel the animal will take. If you are required to wait for assistance before you blood trail, make doubly sure that you have a good mental map of where the animal was standing when you shot, how it reacted to your shot and which direction it traveled.

Terrain can also influence how soon you begin following up your shot. In open terrain, hunters may want to try to stalk closer or intercept the game for a follow-up shot. This is especially true for gun hunters when game goes over a pass or around a butte or down a valley and out of sight. Quickly and quietly stalking closer may give you the opportunity for a quick finishing follow-up shot.

Bowhunters, provided weather conditions are favorable, should avoid following up immediately after the shot. The chance of getting within bow range of a spooked, arrowed animal is rare. If possible, wait for approximately 30 minutes before you begin blood trailing.

Find And Mark The Point Of Impact

Before you begin blood trailing, tie a fluorescent ribbon on your tree stand, ground blind or a nearby tree. This will serve as an easy reference point when you are following the blood trail and look back to confirm the direction you are traveling. It is surprising how difficult it can be to locate your tree stand or ground blind when looking at it from an unfamiliar angle.

The first blood trailing task is to find the location where the animal was standing when you shot and mark it with a piece of toilet paper or flagging tape. If bowhunting, search thoroughly for your arrow. And study any blood and hair you find on the ground, arrow shaft, fletch or broadhead. Hair color and blood composition can help you estimate the point of entrance and exit. (We'll discuss blood color and composition later in this chapter.)

Once you have thoroughly examined that location, proceed slowly step by step in the direction the animal traveled. Look for the next sign of blood. If working with a hunting partner, you should have your partner stay at the previous blood sighting while you look for the next blood sign. If working with a hunting guide, you might want the guide, who may be the more expert blood trailer, to take the lead. When trailing, do not walk on the blood trail. Stay to one side in case you have to retrace your steps.

Mark the location where the animal was standing when you shot, and search thoroughly for any sign. Hair or blood found in this area will help you pinpoint the entrance and exit wounds. This, in turn, can help you anticipate where the animal might travel.

If the blood trail is easy to follow, mark it occasionally with flagging tape or toilet paper. (Whatever you use, be sure to pick it up when you are finished trailing.) Walk quietly and slowly.

As you follow a blood trail, try to determine where the blood is in relation to the animal's trail. Blood on both sides of the trail often indicates a pass-through. Also, blood often will "splatter" or "run" in the direction the animal is moving when the drops hit the ground.

You can often approximate where the animal's wound is located based on the color or composition of the blood. Bright red blood with bubbles often indicates a lung hit. Dark red blood often indicates a liver hit. And blood mixed with visceral material often indicates a gut shot. Even if you don't find any blood, do not give up. Game with just an entrance wound may show little external bleeding. Also, game animals having thick layers of fat or lots of hair—especially black bear—leave a small, hard-to-follow blood trail requiring a slower pace and close inspection.

How To Find A Lost Blood Trail

If you lose the blood trail, mark the last blood spot with highly visible tape. Look back at the trail formed by your markers. You should be able to determine a general direction of travel. If you can, project that line of travel and continue slowly, looking for any blood sign. If there is none, return to the last spot where you found blood.

From the last blood sign begin working outward in a small, spiraling circle. You will have a better chance on your hands and knees of locating any small spot of blood. Slowly spiral out in this way from the last blood sign.

Blood sign that you found earlier may help you predict where a fatally hit game animal may have traveled. Typically, well-hit animals will travel downhill. A gut-shot animal often will head to

Be patient and thorough when following a blood trail. These blood spots, for example, were on the bottom side of these leaves. This sign could have been easily missed. Mark signs like this with flagging tape or toilet paper.

water if there is some within the vicinity.

If you are still unsuccessful, you may want to consider using a product that can make blood fluoresce. Sure Sign—like similar products from other manufacturers—is sprayed on the ground near the last blood sign. Its chemical spray causes the blood to fluoresce. Not only is this product a terrific way to find additional blood sign, it is also a boon to those hunters who are color-confused and cannot see blood's red color. It is estimated that up to 8 percent of all hunters are color-confused, according to figures developed by the late Red Chaplin who helped direct the study that established Hunter Orange as the best protective color for all hunters.

If these techniques still prove unsuccessful, investigate every game trail in the area. Look carefully on each trail for blood sign. You might also ask your hunting buddy for his help.

Because so many big-game animals are active just before dusk, blood trailing after sunset is often unavoidable. In those situations where you know the area well, a Coleman gas lantern is one of the most valuable tools you can keep in your vehicle or at base camp. For some chemical reason, light from a Coleman gas lantern makes blood spots shine—almost glow—like red emeralds. If you've blood trailed at night with a Coleman lantern, you know what we're talking about—especially if you've already tried the near-impossible task of blood trailing with a flashlight.

In unfamiliar terrain or in areas where it can be easy to become disoriented, trailing after dark can spell disaster, leaving you lost, tired and very cold. Get help or let somebody know where you will be and what time you will return. Best course of action is to wait until morning to resume the blood trail. Of course, if it is very warm, the animal could spoil by morning, but you could easily walk right past the animal in the dark and wind up spending a miserable night totally lost. Even if you find the animal, you may not be able to pack the animal out of the woods by yourself—especially if you don't know where you are. If you do decide to wait until morning, leave highly visible markings on the blood trail so it will be easy to pick up and follow the next morning. Whatever you decide, remember it is better to err on the side of caution.

Approaching Downed Game

Approach any downed game with caution. Before you go charging in to claim your trophy, take a moment to make certain it is dead. Every so often we read about a deer hunter who approached a buck only to discover it was still alive. A wrestling match, although rare, sometimes ensues. First check the animal's eyes. A dead animal's eyes will be open. If they are closed, do not approach. This is especially true when hunting more dangerous big game like bear or wild boars. Be very cautious. Toss a stick at the animal. Some bowhunters poke the animal with a broadhead-tipped arrow to make sure it's dead. If you have any doubt, fire another carefully aimed shot into the animal's vitals.

Estimating Live Weight In The Field

NAHC members can estimate the weight of their deer in the field by taking one simple measurement. According to the Wisconsin Department of Natural Resources, that measurement is the chest circumference. Measure just behind the front legs. Then use this chart to determine the approximate weight.

Chest Size (inches)	Live Weight (pounds)	Field Dressed Weight (pounds)
35	136	112
36	145	120
37	156	129
38	166	139
39	178	149
40	204	172
41	210	177
42	218	184
43	234	198
44	250	212
45	267	228

Field Dressing Big Game

Field dress your game animal as soon as possible. Some animals, especially those with thick layers of fat and those in mild to warmer climates, can spoil quickly. If you are bowhunting and did not recover your broadhead or any part of your arrow shaft, be extremely careful when you field dress the animal. The broadhead or part of the arrow shaft may be inside the body cavity.

Here are three simple steps you can follow to field dress your big-game animal:

1. Place the animal on its back and make an incision just below the sternum. Slip two fingers into this cut, pull the hide up and away from the internal organs, and carefully cut down to and around

Field dressing game in the field will help cool the meat and prevent spoilage. Follow the three steps discussed in this chapter to field dress big game. The hunter shown here is at step two.

the sexual organ to the anus. Be careful not to puncture internal organs. Then, go back to the sternum and cut through the abdominal wall from the sternum to the pelvic bone using the same technique. Again, be careful not to puncture any internal organs.

2. Inside the body cavity carefully cut around the diaphragm where it connects to the inside of the body cavity. Reach up into the chest cavity, grab the windpipe and pull it toward you. Cut the windpipe as far forward as you can, being careful not to cut yourself. Pull most of the internal organs out of the body cavity.

3. Inside the abdominal cavity, cut around the large intestine. Be careful not to cut the urethra or the intestine itself. From the outside, cut around the anus and tie it off with a piece of string. From the inside, pull the large intestine and the urethra into the body cavity. Then, drain all blood and remove all remaining organs from the body cavity as quickly as possible.

Some hunters will split the pelvic bone to help cool the hind quarters. Also, many hunters place a stick in the chest cavity to keep that area open and help it cool. Both of these common sense techniques will help keep meat from spoiling.

Caping Your Trophy

Trophy game animals are rare. When you harvest a trophy, a shoulder mount can be your reward for years of hard work. It can be a terrific reminder of fond hunting memories.

As I write this, a shoulder mount of my first Pope & Young animal, a pronghorn, watches over me. Sometimes, I just sit back and look at him and remember. I relive the afternoon when he charged across that South Dakota prairie to run off the little buck decoy I was hiding behind. I remember how he licked his nose so he could smell better; it turned glossy black, then faded to flat brown in the warm September breeze. I remember how he twisted his neck to check on his harem of eight does. I remember all of this and more because of this shoulder mount. For me, it calls forth more memories than any photo.

That evening, after field dressing the animal we began caping the record-book animal. Had it not been for the know-how of Mark Kayser of the South Dakota Department of Tourism, I probably would have blundered the cape or worse. Nobody had ever explained to me the relatively simple process of caping a trophy

Caping your trophy can be accomplished by following the five steps discussed in this chapter. For best results, take more hide to the taxidermist than you think he will need.

buck or bull for a shoulder mount.

How you cape your trophy will determine, in part, the quality of your finished shoulder mount. Here, then, are five simple steps for caping your next trophy buck or bull. This process leaves the delicate task of skinning the head to the taxidermist or your big-game guide.

1. Cut the hide from the base of the sternum straight up to the backbone on both sides. Be sure to start this cut behind the front legs. The finished cut should go completely around the body.

2. Cut around each front leg at armpit level. Then cut from each armpit incision straight back to the sternum cut.

3. Start at the base of the skull and make a cut on the top of the backbone down to the sternum cut.

4. Starting at the sternum cut, separate the hide from the body, pulling the hide up toward the head. Use a knife as required, but be careful not to puncture or slice the hide.

5. Pull hide over the skull as far forward as possible. Cut off the skull and cape at its base near the top of the neck. Store cape in a cool place and deliver to your taxidermist as soon as possible.

Successful big-game recovery is not rocket science, but it is a skill which requires patience and persistence. Follow the guidelines set forth in this chapter. When every piece of your hunting puzzle fits perfectly into place, the result will be a well-deserved smile and a freezer full of tasty meat.

3

The Ideal Big-Game Rifle

by Bob Hagel

Many hunters don't have the budget or the inclination to buy a different rifle for each kind of hunting they do. For that reason, I suppose, I have often been asked to recommend the best all-around cartridge for hunting American big game.

One time in particular, a hunter said he was of the opinion that the .270 Win. is the best. He was, of course, aware that the .270 Win. is not necessarily one of my favorite cartridges under all hunting conditions for all species of North American big-game animals, and that I think it has definite limitations.

To determine what would be the all-around cartridge, we have to ask a few questions. The first one that occurs to me, when someone expresses a preference for one cartridge or another, is how much game has he killed or seen killed with it, and how does it compare with the many other cartridges available to the average hunter? Is this experience based on hunting game that the average American hunter looks for each fall—antelope, deer and black bear—or does it include the larger species like elk, moose and grizzly? And, under what conditions has most of the hunting been done? Has he hunted all kinds of terrain, from the deserts of the Southwest to the timberless tundra of the North to the broken mountain country that lies between, as well as the thick stuff where 50 yards is long-range?

The answers to these questions can and do change opinions on what it takes to be the ideal all-around cartridge. To make a completely candid and objective choice, the hunter has to be thoroughly familiar with hunting all game under all conditions he is likely to encounter in all areas of the country. In addition, the hunting must be done not just with one or two cartridges, but with the many calibers and cartridges of various sizes and ranges of potency available.

For example, take our hunter friend's opinion that the .270 Win. is the top all-around cartridge for hunting American big game. For the fellow who hunts pronghorn on occasion, black bear when the opportunity presents, deer of any kind under any conditions (and especially mule deer wherever they are found), sheep, and goats, as well as caribou (if he happens to hunt on their range), the .270 Win. is hard to beat. For animals in this weight class, it is an ideal all-around cartridge, but certainly no better than several others—the .280 Rem. being one and the .30-06 another. Also, the .270 Win. cleanly kills any game animal in North America, or anywhere in the world for that matter, if the right bullet is used and put in exactly the right spot under ideal conditions. But, that doesn't make it the best choice for an all-around cartridge for all American big game.

No one who does much hunting or shooting needs to be told what my old friend Jack O'Connor thought about the .270 Win. as a big-game cartridge. However, when he hunted Alaskan brown bear on Admiralty Island many years ago, he did not use one of his favorite .270 Win. rifles; he used a .375 H&H Magnum.

One criterion for an all-around cartridge for American big game is that it handles bullets of various weights that are not only suited for shooting pronghorn weighing 100 pounds or so, but for Alaskan-Yukon moose, weighing as much as a ton, as well as brownies that are close up in the brush and can rough you up if not put out of commission with the first shot—all within reasonable hunting ranges. It should also be able to do the job under conditions in which the animal is not posing in picture-book broadside position. And let's not be seduced by the oft-repeated saying that the good, experienced hunter does not shoot unless everything is exactly right—because 98 percent do!

For these reasons, I would personally prefer either the .280 Rem. or the .30-06 to the .270 Win. as an all-around cartridge for hunting American big game. The .280 Rem. shoots just as flat with the lighter bullets for long-range work on smaller species and offers heavier bullets for deeper penetration on the big ones. The

For animals in the same weight class as this pronghorn, the .270 Win., .280 Rem. and .30-06 are ideal cartridges. However, the correct bullet needs to be used and conditions need to be good.

.30-06 is almost as flat as either one with light bullets (just as flat if loaded to the same pressures) and has the advantage of the real heavyweights like the 200 and 220-grain for heavy game at close range. It also has the advantage of a larger frontal area that does more tearing along the way.

That's not to say that any one of these is the ideal all-around cartridge. There are cartridges that not only shoot the lighter bullets in their respective calibers flatter, but also shoot the heavier bullets just as flat as the .280 or the .30-06 can shoot the light ones. For this reason, they are much better suited for shooting elk and moose at longer distances. The various 7mm Magnum cartridges shoot 150- or 160-grain bullets at about the same velocity as the .270 Win. does the 130-grain, and the .300 Magnums do the same thing with the 165- to 180-grain bullets. The big sevens and .30s also carry the heavyweight 175-grain, 7mm and the 200- and 220-grain, .308 bullets for the big stuff at any effective range.

Moving up the caliber ladder, we find the .338 Win. Mag. and the .340 Wthby. On the heavy end, bullets from 250 to 300 grains are available for adequate bone-shattering penetration—bullets that will quickly put a moose down. Even these heavy bullets move along fast enough to make fatal shots on larger animals fairly easy at practical ranges. For the flattest trajectory when shooting the smaller species like pronghorn, sheep, goat and deer at long range without too much guesswork, the 200- and 210-grain bullets in the .340 Wthby drop no more than the 130-grain from the .270 Win., and the .338 Win. is not far behind.

Sure, I know the .340 Wthby is not an ideal pronghorn cartridge, and that the .270 Win., .280 Rem., .30-06 and a host of other cartridges are better choices. I also know that the .340 will surely kill the pronghorn. If you think it is "overkill," I can't see it as a fault. But, I wouldn't be overly happy trailing a wounded brownie (or even if he weren't wounded) into the thick stuff along an Alaskan salmon creek with a .270 Win. If you polled Alaskan guides on the cartridges used on brown-bear hunts, you'll find most would agree. But, if you think I firmly believe the .338 Win. Mag. and .340 Wthby Mag. are the best all-around cartridges, that isn't correct, either.

Considering the various species of big game hunted in North America, the conditions they are hunted under in various places and times, the sizes and temperaments of those animals, and the fact that the hunter may have only one opportunity to take a certain animal on a very expensive trip, it is not hard to arrive at the conclusion that there is *no single best* all-around cartridge. I've shot game with most of the commercial numbers and a lot of wildcats, but when I'm on a hunt that requires a lot of time, effort and dollars, I choose a cartridge that I think will do the best job for the kind of game being hunted in the area where it lives. And I don't worry much about whether it is considered an all-around cartridge. I do, however, prefer "overkill" to "underkill."

Sizing Up The Ideal Rifle

With the advance of technology in all lines of endeavor since this country was first colonized, it would seem that life would steadily become less complicated with decisions easier to make and greater opportunity to attain the ideal answers to our needs. But it doesn't always work out that way.

Take hunting with firearms, for example. Our forefathers lived off the land by necessity, and hunting was at least as important as any other aspect of living. But the choice of firearms was simple because the only guns were muzzleloaders that were about as long as a fence post and almost as heavy. The diameter of the balls that they fired varied, but most were large. These rifles were cumbersome by any standard, but people of the frontier were used to doing things for themselves with whatever they had at hand. The settler's hunting rifle was no exception.

The American hunting rifle remained about the same until the advent of the metallic cartridge. That is, the rifle was loaded from the front and was long, heavy and ungainly. Of course, some improvements in ballistic performance came with the introduction of rifled bores and conical bullets like the hollow-base pointed Minie ball.

When the first metallic cartridges did appear, and repeating rifles like the Spencer and Henry were designed to handle them, the hunting rifle took a new turn in portability. But while the new repeaters were lighter and shorter than the muzzleloader, making them a lot easier to pack in the hand or on the side of a horse, the cartridges that they fired were rather puny against the larger, big-game animals of the Western frontier. The repeater's advantage in firepower was more than offset by the lack of effectiveness in killing larger game like elk, moose, buffalo and grizzly bear.

With lever-action repeaters chambering only cartridges of inadequate power for larger big game and capable only of close-range shooting of smaller species, big-bore cartridges holding

Although heavy and cumbersome, the Winchester Model 1895 rode well in a saddle scabbard and was considered the ideal, all-around big-game rifle of its day by many big-game hunters. It was chambered for some of the most powerful and flat-shooting cartridges that were popular then, such as the .35 and .405 Win., the .30-40 Krag and the .30-03 (later .30-06).

large charges of black powder behind long, heavy bullets became more popular, even though the single-shot rifles that fired them were often long and heavy. The big-game hunter, who was often a market hunter for hides or meat, needed a rifle that he could depend on to give sure kills at both short and long ranges. He was a tough and hardy realist who preferred a cartridge with sure killing ability to a light, short, handy rifle. His livelihood depended upon accuracy and killing power, not on the ease of packing the rifle.

It was not until the 1880s that the repeating rifle started to take over as the ideal, all-around rifle for hunting American big game. When John Browning designed the action that became the Model 1886 Winchester, it not only set a precedent in lever-action design, but allowed the chambering of black-powder cartridges which were effective on all types of American game.

The Model 1886 was followed by other Winchester lever actions of similar design, including the famous Model 1894, which is still going strong over 90 years later. Two factors added to the popularity of the Model 94: The light, short carbine fit so well on the saddle that you hardly knew it was there, and it was chambered for the new small-caliber cartridges that were charged with smokeless powder.

Marlin produced similar lever-action rifles chambered for some of the same cartridges, or for similar Marlin types. Savage came along with the Model 99 with its rotary magazine that eliminated the magazine tube under the barrel and improved the aesthetics.

By the early 1890s, smokeless-powder cartridges were becoming popular, and the lever actions of 1870 to 1890 vintage were either not strong enough or too short to handle some of the modern cartridges. This probably influenced the development of the Browning-designed, 1895 Winchester lever action with its in-line magazine under the receiver. This rifle was chambered for some of the most powerful, smokeless cartridges of the day: the .30-40 Krag, .35 Win. and .405 Win., and eventually the .30-03 and .30-06, as well as other smokeless and black-powder cartridges.

The Model 95 was made in several versions with barrels of different lengths and styles. And while it was heavy and a bit cumbersome with the magazine protruding under the receiver, it was considered by many experienced hunters as the ideal all-around, big-game rifle. Teddy Roosevelt considered it the best big-game rifle that he had ever used, and it became very popular in the Alaska-Yukon gold-rush country. The cartridges that it fired were probably more responsible for its popularity and reputation as an ideal big-game rifle than the rifle itself.

This period saw the popularity peak of the lever action as the

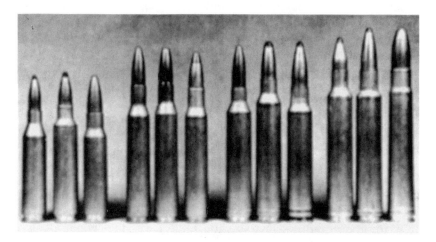

Cartridge length governs the suitability of rifle actions for their cartridges. In the first group (left): the .243, 284 and .308 Win. function in lever-action and short-bolt-action rifles. Standard-length cartridges in the second group: the 270 Win., 7mm Express Remington and .30-06 require longer rifle actions; so do the short magnums in the third group: 7mm Rem. Mag., .300 Win. Mag. and .338 Win. Mag. The longest cartridges: the .300 and .340 Wthby Mag. and the .375 H&H Mag., are suitable for only the longest actions.

ideal big-game hunting arm. The development of the strong bolt action and the high-pressure cartridges that followed ruled out the use of the weaker, rear-lockup lever action as a base for the ideal big-game rifle.

The first bolt-action rifles that could be considered anything like ideal big-game rifles sprung from military actions—the Krag, Mauser and Springfield. In some cases, the military rifles themselves were kept almost entirely, with the stocks simply worked over by removing the excess wood and sometimes inlaying extra wood to form a pistol grip and raise the comb. Other rifles were restocked to give dimensions more suited to the bolt action and to the use of the telescopic sights that were starting to appear in sizes and weights that could be used for hunting big game. Custom gunsmithing shops sprang up all around the country and turned out many rifles that were considered ideal, all-around big-game rifles. Most of those rifles had 24-inch barrels, while some had 22-inch barrels. Weight was held down to 8 pounds or so with iron sights. These rifles handled and carried well, and were chambered for high-velocity cartridges ranging from the .250-3000 Savage to the .30-06.

The hunting rifle situation didn't change much until the 1920s when Remington updated the old 1917 Enfield action into the Model 30 and 30S, and Winchester came along with the Model 54. The Model 54 Winchester was seen by many big-game hunters as the ultimate big-game rifle, and that thought carried over to the Model 70 when it replaced the Model 54 in 1935. The Remington Model 721 also had many fans who remained loyal until the Model 700 arrived to become one of the most popular big-game rifles made anywhere.

Until World War II, about the only change that had much effect on rifles ideally suited to hunting American big game was when Winchester chambered the Model 70 for the .300 H&H and .375 H&H Magnum cartridges in 1937. These two British cartridges not only became quite popular with American hunters, but paved the way for later American developments of magnum cases. The thinking then (and it's just as valid today) was that when using a magnum cartridge, a long barrel was necessary to burn the big powder charge efficiently. Also, the barrel's extra length added weight which reduced muzzle jump and muzzle blast, making felt recoil less objectionable.

Then things started to change in the early 1950s with a trend toward ultra-light, short rifles. It is hard to say whether the

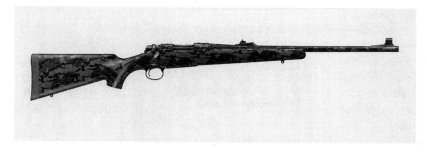

A long-action rifle, such as this Remington Model 700 Mountain Rifle (top), will weigh about 3 ounces more and is 1 inch longer than a short-action rifle, such as this Remington Model 700 CS Camo Synthetic (bottom). However, the major difference will be in the chambering for cartridges.

American big-game hunter suddenly lost the stamina to carry anything besides himself through the woods and up mountains, or whether modern living created the impression that any physical exertion and discomfort should be avoided—no matter what the cost in efficiency.

In the frenzied search for lighter and shorter rifles, any barrel length over 22 inches was a major sin, and an action long enough to handle anything longer than the .30-06 case was to be avoided completely. From this sprang a line of short magnums including the .264 Win., .338 Win. and .458 Win., and, a bit later, the 7mm Rem. Mag. and .300 Win. However, all of this turned out quite well, because these short-belted cases with their minimum body taper had as much powder capacity as the much longer H&H cases.

In fact, the howl for even lighter and shorter rifles became so loud that Remington developed the 6.5mm and .350 Rem. Mag. cartridges especially for the Remington Model 600 with its very short action and 18½-inch barrel. The rifle's total length was 37½ inches, and it weighed just over 6 pounds.

The short, fat cases actually have about the same powder capacity as the .30-06, but not when bullets for the 6.5mm and .350 cartridges have to be seated to fit the short action and magazine of the Model 600. Many bullets would not hold in the short neck of the 6.5mm when handloaded to fit the magazine, and the heavier bullets greatly cut into powder capacity. This, coupled with the short, 18½-inch barrel, dropped ballistic performance so much that even the hunters who were obsessed with shorter, lighter rifles could see that it had gone too far. Of course, Remington was the loser because the Model 600 and the later Model 660 were discontinued.

Meanwhile, Winchester discovered that while the Model 70 Featherweight sold very well with its 22-inch barrel in standard calibers, it was a classic flop when chambered for the .264 Win. Mag. With 4 inches chopped off the barrel, the high-velocity, flat-shooting .264 Win. Mag. was not far ahead of the .270 Win. with the same barrel length, and it kicked up a lot more muzzle blast and jump, along with a harder punch to the shoulder.

It would seem that the marketing failure of short-barreled, light rifles when chambered for magnum cartridges would have taught big-game hunters a lesson in cartridge efficiency vs. rifle portability. But if my mail, phone calls and personal contacts mean anything, it didn't. Some of the older hunters either have short memories or never used the big cartridges. Many of the younger hunters apparently haven't looked very far back into the history of big-game rifles and cartridges. Something worth considering is that few, if any, commercial rifles with magnum chambers are sold today with barrels shorter than 24 inches. In fact, some have 26-inch barrels as an option.

The short, light rifles are fine if you prefer to use the so-called standard cartridges in the power range of the .270 Win., the .280 Rem. or the .30-06. The 22-inch barrels that are so popular on today's rifles in these calibers do not give as much velocity as the 24-inch barrels, but they lose only about 50 fps, which isn't an overly important loss. If you want to reduce weight and length to even lower levels, you can always settle for the cartridges made to function through the short actions designed for the .308 cartridge length. You will, of course, have to settle for cartridges like the 7mm-08, .308, .358 and a few others. The rifle will be short, light and easy to carry up a mountain, but few hunters consider any of

From left: a Ruger M77 in .338 Win. Mag., a custom-stocked Remington 700 in 6mm Rem., and a Remington 700 Mountain Rifle in .280 Rem. This trio provides appropriate calibers and designs to cover all types of North American big-game hunting.

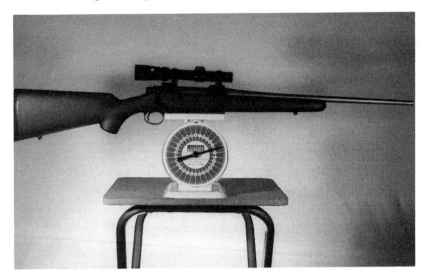

For those who insist on having the lightest, shortest rifles for hunting big game, the fiberglass stock and the ultra-light 20-inch barrel of the Brown High Country Rifle should meet with approval. Although this barrel does well when chambered for the .270 Win., it is questionable when chambered for a short magnum.

these cartridges ideal for all-around hunting of American big game.

The old adage, "You can't have your cake and eat it, too," is as true with rifles as anything else; you have to compromise, and the ideal rifle-and-cartridge combination requires sacrifice.

As far as rifle design is concerned, there are several angles to consider for what *you* consider the ideal, all-around, big-game rifle. First, there's the rifle's action. Regarding the very short and light action that will be chambered for the short cartridges just mentioned, the Remington Model 700 short action weighs about 3 ounces less than the long action that can handle everything up to, and including, the .375 H&H and Weatherby magnums, and it is ¾ inch shorter. So, assuming that you use the same barrel length and weight, a rifle made on the short action weighs only 3 ounces less and is less than an inch shorter than one with the long action. This isn't really a lot of saving with a light, short rifle. The major difference is in the chambering for cartridges. The short action handles only cartridges that are minimal for all-around big-game shooting, but the long action handles all the standard-length cartridges like the .30-06, as well as the short and long magnum cases with the exception of the .378 and .460 Weatherby case which is too fat, but not too long. Obviously, the short action is not the ideal base for the ideal, all-around, big-game rifle—this applies to all short actions, not just Remington's.

So the long action is chosen for the ideal rifle. It doesn't necessarily have to accept the long magnum cartridges, as do the long Remington Model 700, Winchester Model 70, Sako magnum-length, and some others; but it should accept .30-06-length cartridges and the short magnums up to the .300 Win. As we've seen, this action is a bit longer and heavier, so to make it light and short, the barrel must be chopped to no more than 22 inches and thinned as much as possible. The action can also be lightened by milling and drilling here and there, and the stock can be hollowed out in the front and in the butt. This drops the weight a pound or so and makes the rifle reasonably short. If you want to go all the way, you can put on a fiberglass stock and drop the weight about another pound. In fact, the High Country rifle made by Brown Precision uses only a 20-inch barrel that has a muzzle diameter under ½ inch and weighs just over 6 pounds, complete with a light scope and mount when built on the long Model 700 action and chambered for the .270 Win.

A lot of hunters will ask what they have really given up if such a rifle will handle the standard cartridges, as well as the very efficient short magnums. The answer is that they won't give up too much, as long as they stick to the standard-capacity cases. The .270 Win. loses very little velocity in a 22-inch barrel, as compared to a 24-inch barrel, and not a great deal more from a 20-inch barrel. The .280 Rem. and .30-06 do not do as well in short barrels as the .270 Win. for some reason, but they still do quite well in velocity.

However, a lot of hunters today lean toward magnum cartridges that shoot flatter and pack more punch at long ranges and some that use heavy, large-caliber bullets that take care of the heavy game at all ranges. Short, light rifles and magnum cartridges don't mix very well. Not only does velocity go down with big cases that burn a lot of slow powder when barrel length drops below 24 inches, but recoil becomes unbearable for many shooters. If you want a short, light rifle, you don't want it chambered for a magnum cartridge, and if you prefer a magnum cartridge, you don't want it chambered in a light rifle with a short barrel.

When thinking about the ideal rifle for all-around big-game hunting, which should be as light as possible while still being efficient, think about the scope. I've seen dozens of hunters climbing mountains with the lightest and shortest rifles available, yet mounted with a scope nearly as long and heavy as the rifle. These scopes are, of course, big variables of at least 3-9X, and some are even larger. These fellows apparently don't realize that they have undone most of what they tried to accomplish with their ideal hunting rifles. The big scope is so bulky and heavy that it is prone to lose its zero when subjected to hard, rough use. It adds much weight and cumbersome bulk to the rifle, is difficult to carry, and its higher power range isn't needed for hunting big game. A scope of no more than 4X and as short and light as possible is the best all-around, big-game scope available. If you can't see a big-game animal well enough to hit it with a good 4X hunting scope, that animal is too far away to shoot at.

Summing Up

In summing up the discussion of the ideal all-around, big-game rifle, I have rifles with barrels from 18½ to 26 inches, and some with .500-inch-diameter muzzles and some that mike .700 inch. Some actions are short, some are long, and some rifles have been skeletonized here and there to cut weight while retaining efficiency. But the cartridge is always suited to the rifle. So, in reality, it becomes the best-suited combination for hunting big-game animals.

4

Fifty Techniques For Mule Deer

by Wayne van Zwoll

Most magazine articles about deer hunting tell you two ways to hunt on your own: stand-hunting (sitting still) or still-hunting (moving slowly). It's okay to describe whitetail hunting this way, but mule deer country is more diverse, often much more open and calls for a different and more flexible approach. The best way to hunt mule deer on your own is to combine stand- and still-hunting with glassing and stalking.

A few people have rattled mule deer in, but generally rattling is not as productive with mule deer as with whitetail. Rattling works best during the short rut season. It's ill suited to open country or where you want to stay a distance from the deer. In whitetail coverts you are right in with the deer, and any place where you can be that close is likely a good place to rattle.

In the mountains you may have to work across terrain where you don't expect to find deer while looking across a drainage or up a slope where you do. To rattle where deer don't normally go is foolish; to penetrate the areas that you could hunt from a distance in order to rattle will push deer out and away from you. Mule deer will leave cover if you disturb them. Still-hunting justifies the risk of moving deer out. Rattling does not.

So you can see that mule deer hunting is often different from pursuing whitetails. How do we come up with techniques that will work on mule deer territory?

There's a lot about hunting that you learn only by doing. You don't have to kill to learn. In fact, you may learn most when you don't kill, because you spend more time in the field. Learning means that you stay alert and keep your mind open to new thoughts. It's a good idea to have a notebook of things you want to remember. Mine is a 6x9-inch spiral notebook; it cost 49 cents. It is the best hunting-equipment bargain I've found. Like a diary, it must be used to be advantageous.

During the past several years, I've developed a list of ideas that work for me. I suspect many will work for you. Some won't, perhaps, because you choose to hunt blacktail and mule deer differently. But you might use these ideas to start a notebook of your own. When I started hunting, I wish I would have had a list like this. They aren't as fun to read as stories about someone's hunting experience, but they will give tips on what you can do to better your own skills.

To show you where ideas like this come from, let's hunt for a few minutes. During the course of the hunt, my companion and I will be using many of the techniques from my spiral notebook. See how many of them you already know, and how many you can come up with while you read the narrative. I'll list a lot of them later in the chapter.

We'll start before dawn from a camp that is high up in mountain country. We could be in Colorado or Montana or Oregon. We might be at 6,000 or 10,000 feet. Based on the vegetation and sign, you've determined that there are deer here. You've looked at the plants, water sources and trails before the season started. You've now read the sign, doped the wind and figured out a plan. Let's hunt.

The camp is down from the rims, sheltered from weather and the eyes of deer. It's been a quiet camp, just us whispering and talking low. The fire was a luxury here (of little concern to the deer). This morning our clothes and bodies are as clean as possible, and we'll be careful not to push ourselves to a sweat as we climb.

We climb when the sky is still black, an iron gray to the east. There's no yellow, pink or even a touch of white. The light is something that's leaking from far away, diffused thinly. If it were light enough to see cross hairs against the brightest part of the sky, we would be too late.

But we're on time with full canteens, loaded rifles and fanny packs plump with the needs of the day. Binoculars bang our chests a little, even though we've tightened the straps with a knot. And

Hunting mule deer can be quite different from hunting whitetails. If hunting for mule deer alone, combine stand- and still-hunting, as well as glassing and stalking.

we've made sure to thoroughly clean the glass for best results.

It's cold. The frost is thick on the ground. We shiver because our coats hang from our waists. In just a few yards we know we will be warm. Hills warm you quickly.

We climb into the thermal drag. There isn't much of it now, just a sense of settling. Last night it was strong. There's a trail that's hard to find but we don't use lights. We prefer to go slow and stumble a bit. This is something we had thought about and planned. We have the time.

It's an hour's climb, and just below ridgeline we rest. The iron gray has turned white, and then there was a pink streak and now there's a little yellow leaking. The black has weakened even in the west, but the half moon is still bright. The stars have left us and you can see cross hairs in the sky.

Our breathing is back to normal. The wind is puffing at our bodies. We let ourselves shiver to dry any dampness, then put on our coats. We won't be moving much for a while. We check the safeties, the glass. The rifles we've had on our shoulders are in our hands.

We creep to the top and peer over. The bush we've chosen on the crest will keep our heads hidden and cover us as we become part of the ridge.

It's hard not to look at the sky, it's so lovely. We'd be missing something if we didn't. So we do, briefly. Then we look down into the gut of the basin that is in front of us, into the dark timber that will again dilate our pupils so we can see detail. Before we raise our binoculars we look carefully without them, from near to far, from the basin head down. We look for movement, for off-white patches and solid blobs of darkness that are deer. We don't see any, not for sure anyway.

Now we glass. Sitting on the ridge, we'd be skylined were it not for the bush at our backs. I look one way, you the other. We glass slowly, you in a grid pattern. I know the grid is the best way to glass but I don't do it because I don't like it. My way is like the chocolate swirl in an ice cream cone that's mostly vanilla. It's not a very neat pattern to watch, but I cover most of the ground and almost as well as you. Both of us stop moving our binoculars frequently, letting our eyes move in a field that's still. Then we slightly shift the glass again. Our elbows are on our knees and it's pretty easy to hold the glasses steady with both hands.

In 15 minutes we're both tired and getting cold. The wind is puffing stronger and each puff is longer. The sun isn't up, but the sky is bright and its colors vibrant. You can see cross hairs in the trees. We lower the glasses and rest, then continue. It's easy just to glance at things or gaze. Our job is to inspect, scrutinize.

That's work. Hunting is work. To hunt well you must put a lot of effort into it.

Another few minutes and the fire of the sun pierces a cut in the distant mountains. It will be a glorious day. I shiver with anticipation. You say, "There's a deer." It didn't just get there. It was there and we'd looked past it several times. It's far away, maybe 450 yards, feeding up from the bottom near the basin head to our right. It's pretty much in the open, and with glasses we can see antlers. It's not a big buck. You ask if I want to stalk him and I say no. You glass the buck again, then pick apart the surrounding cover, the bushes and little trees and big rocks.

"There's another one."

This one is a bigger deer. I can tell without looking at the antlers. His chest is deep and blocky and he looks more masculine than the yearling or 2-year-old above him.

"You saw him, you take him," I whisper back. Nobody's feeling the cold now.

"It's too far. I'll stalk." There's no arguing. The time for being polite or talking about who is going to shoot is before you see a deer.

You glass a little more to find landmarks. "I'll do this myself," you whisper. I nod as you drop quietly behind the bush and over the rim to the trail that threads the shaded side; the side we came up. I could signal directions and make things easier, but easier isn't always better.

The deer move faster as the sun rolls up a mountain. They like its warmth but they want to bed. Still foraging, they walk slowly through the bushes, nibbling here and there. Their tails flick and their ears flip back and forth to catch the morning sounds. Once in a while they stop foraging to raise their heads and look. I see through the glasses that they sniff. I hope you have the wind.

You do, and you're trying to keep it. You move fast but quietly. You must get there before the deer decide to move with a purpose to bed. You've charted only their foraging route and will catch them only if they slowly follow that route. You are stalking blind because the ridge between you and the deer offers you protection from the wind. It screens you and muffles your sounds. This is to your advantage.

When you come on the ridge again you'll shoot.

But the deer are alert to something: maybe you, maybe just the idea that it's time to bed. Both heads are up now. The deer begin to move purposefully and stiff-legged away from the ridge and across the basin head to the dense scrub on the opposite slope.

You see them as you top the ridge, move in front of a bush and sit down, getting into your sling. Your pulse is too fast and you wait as the taut sling battles the jiggling cross hairs. The deer are 300 yards or so but headed directly away from you. Now they're weaving among trees and rocks. When they stop the angle is wrong and they don't stop long. Everything is loose, sloppy. You could shoot and hit the big deer. But you don't feel that tight feeling, the feeling that you're in control and can direct your bullet precisely. You don't shoot.

The sun's up when you return and I know before you tell me what happened because I saw most of it. We walk on a deer trail just below ridgeline on the sunny slope. We'll head down a bit

When glassing for your big-game animal, the grid pattern works best overall. However, some hunters develop personal patterns that work better for them.

toward the timber where other animals might still be up and moving about in the shade of trees in small openings. Because we glassed this area well, there's little chance another deer is in the upper part of this basin. The deer trail lets us walk quietly; the deer expect to hear little sounds and see movement.

One-quarter mile farther we're at the edge of the trees, glassing again. We eat raisins and bagels and drink some water. We let the sun loosen our muscles. In the canyon below, the thermals are lifting. We can see that and feel it. Still-hunting across the slope should be productive. We agree to separate.

I go low and you go high. Each step is slow, deliberate. I walk pretty evenly with a short but definite pause after almost every step. You stop longer and less frequently. We go about the same speed. All the time we look. The cover here isn't thick. Still, a deer can hide in very little cover, and unless it thinks you've seen it, it will often stay motionless and let you pass. People think mule deer bounce out when you get close. This is because the deer that bounce out are the only deer they see. I remember the time on this very ridge I walked past a fine buck as he stood motionless. I saw his throat patch as I turned but kept walking to appear fooled. When I stopped I was ready to shoot and did.

You don't see the deer that bounces out. You know there's no sense in following. You wait a few minutes, counting so you don't cheat on the time, then move on. You must look more carefully. You do, and in 30 minutes you see the horizontal belly line of a deer as you stoop to peer under a juniper. The horizontal lines of a deer are easier to see than the deer.

For many seconds you balance in your position. Even though you are uncomfortable, you want to determine this deer's identity before it breaks. The wind comes then, canceling the thermal and splashing your scent to the deer. It crashes off and you see nothing but its tail.

We get together around lunchtime on the ridge we'd climbed at dawn. It's a good place to meet, and an easy one in midday because you can glass the country. If time is lost getting together it's not so critical at noon—especially in a good glassing spot. We don't commit to meeting (ever) except at camp at night. There are too many things that can draw us apart during the day. Neither of us would compromise a hunt to get together. Loose arrangements are okay.

This time we saw few deer and had no shots. We kept to the trails, mostly with the sun behind us and the wind to our sides. We hunted good cover as best we could. We learned a little more about the cover and the country and about looking for deer and walking slow. That will help us on later hunts.

Now we talk about the afternoon. You decide to explore and hike a bit while glassing likely bedding spots now and then. I'll do the same in another drainage. We part.

Your pace is steady—a stride. It's fast but not quick. You're still careful where you step and are aware of what's around you. The sun and exercise warm you quickly. You stop or slow down before you sweat. You walk just off ridgeline on deer trails, and stop next to a bush or tree to blend with its vertical form. At each stop you glass, trying hard to concentrate. You drink a lot of water even when you're not thirsty.

About the time the sun turns red you've seen plenty of deer country and only one deer. But you saw that one, a little buck, unalarmed in its bed at the base of a cliff.

With all but west-facing basins in shadow now, you decide to move downslope to timber's edge to watch a stringer meadow with lots of trails crossing it. The seep at its base will attract deer. You sit down with your back to a tree just west of the slide. Thermals will switch soon, dragging down. You'll alert deer if you stay above the meadow. You can't see very far, but far enough in most directions to take advantage of what little light you'll have. Watching lots of country just before dark is silly because you'll have no time to stalk distant bucks and insufficient light to see beyond rifle range.

You're shivering by the time you leave. A doe and her fawn have drunk from the seep. That's all you've seen. It's a couple miles back to camp and you walk it as quickly as you can, using your flashlight in the timber. A stiff wind has come up and clouds have curtained the moon and stars.

You make it back to camp, eat a good supper and sleep.

In the morning there is snow, more than you'd have expected this early in the year. We get going at the same time and make the same hike up the ridge because we know it's a good spot. What we did or didn't see yesterday matters little. Sometimes you need faith in yourself and in previous scouting and hunting trips that were productive. Unless we have reason to think the deer have moved, we'll rely on what we know.

The snow is not heavy enough to have moved deer, at least not this early in the season. Later a light snow would signal migration. Now it's just snow. For us, though, it's a great option. Today we can track! And we can move more quickly and quietly.

The glassing we did yesterday can't be done today because there's a cloud in the basin. In the dark we saw it and hoped for the sun. But the sky is overcast now. When it did get light it happened suddenly, as it does on overcast days. Still the clouds stuck to the mountains.

We split up again. The inch of snow won't last if the sun comes out, but we can use it now. Better that we go far from each other so as not to cross tracks. I go into this basin; you head for the country you explored yesterday afternoon.

You move fast along the ridge at first, looking with your binoculars into the basins on either side for deer. The places on rocks and trees where the snow has not stuck are dark, making the scenery speckled. It's hard to spot a deer in patchy snow because neither the white rump nor the brown body stand out. If you were glassing you'd take even more time and do it more slowly than you

Hunting in snow and heavy frost is productive because you can tell fresh tracks from old tracks. It's also easier to pick out deer against the white landscape.

did yesterday. But now you are looking for tracks, keeping your eyes to the basins so you won't miss the obvious deer, the one that is moving.

You stop and take a compass reading, just in case the clouds move in. Then you glass a snowy slope below a saddle on a ridge that meets yours. A deer would be pretty obvious on this big white slide; but you're looking for something more specific. You're using the binoculars to find tracks in a likely place. Saddles are the easiest place to see fresh tracks in the high country, and they're one of the most easy places to find.

You find them here. They're faint streaks from a distance. If the snow had been there a while there might have been places that snowballs had tumbled down the slide. But this is fresh snow and still cold. In 15 minutes you're standing by the tracks.

They're well defined because the snow is not powdery. It was heavy as it fell, wet and sticky, and takes a print nicely. These tracks are big. There's only one set. The toes are blunt and the prints are well off centerline. While there are big does that travel alone and have hooves worn blunt by the rocks, the firm print of the dewclaws and the wide lateral spacing of the tracks makes you think this is a mature buck.

There is no way to tell the tracks of immature bucks from those of does, and sexing any track is risky. The mature mule deer buck is wide-chested and heavy, and often drags his feet. There are no drag marks here, but the snow is not deep enough. The other evidence suggests a big buck. You take the track into the basin.

Because the snow is new you know this is a fresh trail. If the snow stays the same temperature for several days it's hard to tell which tracks are fresh. You remember when I hunted where there were many fresh-looking tracks but few deer. The reason was that the snow had been the same temperature for six days. It had fallen late in the season after a very dry fall and about the time mule deer were rutting. Right after the storm, deer had moved around, eating, migrating, mating. By the time I saw the tracks, the few deer that made them had moved to lower country.

You watch ahead as you walk just to the side of the track, careful not to spoil it because you may want to look at it again. Mule deer sometimes circle if they know they're being followed, walking back on the tracks they've made. Your boot prints there would make things hard to straighten out. Another reason you walk to the side is to avoid being spotted by the deer. The buck will probably keep alert to things behind him, especially what's happening on his trail—it's instinct.

You walk briskly at first because the buck is traveling at a fast walk, not foraging. His trail winds down the slope into thick timber, then back up into scattered bushes. It's a purposeful trail but not as straight-line and purposeful as a deer on the move to winter range. This is the kind of track a deer lays every night up here. Only now you can see it.

There's an anticipation in trailing a buck that's hard to understand by watching from a stand or while still-hunting. You know he's in front of you. You don't know where, but you know the tracks will lead you to him. It's exciting! You feel that excitement now as you skirt a steep rim, then plunge into the big timber opposite the saddle. He likes this drainage—you think.

The tracks are spaced closer now and you see where the deer has nibbled. You cross another set of tracks, and another. One looks as big as the set you're on and it's headed into the open country on the ridges. You'd like to take it, but jumping from one track to another is seldom a good idea. You refrain.

Soon you notice the track is leading you deeper into timber, across the basin, on an angle with the drainage. You stop for a compass reading, then go on. Another track joins the trail you follow. It was made by a smaller deer. Later it diverges. Now the prints are closer together and the trail twists. The timber is thick and you hope the buck has chosen another place to bed, a place you can survey before he knows you're there. With no wind today, a damp, steely cold hangs from the sky. If the wind were puffing you'd have to figure how to come in against it. With the tracks snaking here and there, it appears that the buck has started to look for a bed. If he's close, the wind is important. Until now you've ignored it.

As the buck has slowed, you slow, peering through the trees, staying as far to the side of the track as you can without losing it. Suddenly there is a rockslide in front of you, an opening. You move forward cautiously. The trail straightens out and angles up the slide. You glass what rim you can see before you leave the trees. Then you climb.

Here the buck moves powerfully, with something in mind. It isn't a trot; the jagged rubble won't permit that. But something about the track tells you that he's alerted. You climb fast, right on the track because there's only a narrow path across the slide. On dirt again, the deer trots, confirming what you suspect. He heads across the slope. You follow.

You cannot tell buck tracks from doe tracks if both are of normal size. Big bucks can leave tracks that are bigger than any doe's, and the prints are wide from centerline, suggesting a broader chest. The toes are often rounded like these.

There is rough country ahead and on impulse you abandon the track and climb. If you can see beyond the fingers coming off this basin's side perhaps you can spot the deer before it penetrates the thick new-growth conifers on the bench ahead.

You haven't much time, if any. For all you know the deer is in the conifers now. But if it was just a few yards ahead at the rockslide you may be close enough.

There's a rock above you, a big one. You'll be able to see off it. You're sweating in the cold, but there's a time to worry about sweat and a time to sweat. You climb faster, careful not to let your breath hit your binocular lenses. If they fog now you'll not have time to clear them.

Just below the rock you stop to catch your breath. No matter the time, if you can't hold your binoculars or rifle steady the deer is safe. Slowly you peek around the rock, trying to see deer on the fingers between you and the conifer bench a quarter mile away.

There's still no wind, and while the clouds have inched up out of the basins they're still tight around the peaks, and the sky foretells more snow.

There's no deer in front of you. You make sure of that before turning to the opposite side of the canyon. After you turn, you see three deer right away. You can tell they're not big bucks by their body shape. In the binoculars and against the snow they become two does and a forkhorn. You look other places for deer, check the fingers in front again, then get out some peanuts and raisins. You drink, too, more than you want because it's cold. After you're done you put your coat on to ward off the chill of your own sweat, then you glass the snow on either side of the conifers. You can see no tracks.

About the only thing left to do is descend the slope to the trail again and continue on. You don't like that idea because losing and gaining elevation is hard. Dropping to the track and stepping quickly along it you notice it turns down toward the timber. The climb was for nothing! Now you wonder in disgust if one of the deer you saw on the other side of the canyon made these tracks. A doe or young buck after all that work! But you know you think that because you're tired, and you know that second-guessing has no place in hunting. A hunch works for you sometimes, but not a double mind.

The track stops short of the trees and winds along the foot of the slope below the bench with the conifers. The deer is not trotting now; it's running! No doubt it saw you come out of the timber and start climbing. Then it came down behind a fold in the slope. Perhaps as you glassed it was watching from below—the only place you didn't look.

You run after this deer as best you can, then slow to a brisk walk as the terrain gets tough. Beyond the bench, the deer climbs again, slowing to that purposeful walk. The trail leads you over the rocks and through stunted aspens and low brush. You stop and look at your watch. Four o'clock! In an hour and a half it will be dark, and you're two hours from camp.

Before you abandon the track, though, you climb again, just above it, to look. This time there's nothing, even across canyon. Instead of dropping back down you angle up toward ridgetop. You'll walk the rim to camp. It's easier up there, and shorter. Half an hour later you crest the ridge.

On the other side is a basin, gloomy and rough-looking and turning darker with time. There is no sun but there's an "evening look'' to things. You scan the basin without binoculars. This time you look down; this time you see a buck.

He's not at the base of the slope which is hundreds of yards away, rather he is just below you—maybe 50 yards away. As you swing your rifle up he bounds downslope. The antlers are big and the back and neck are broad. He runs heavily. The cross hairs dance back and forth and you know it's hopeless unless he stops. You're too winded to shoot offhand even at a still target.

It's unlikely he'll stop, though. Mule deer often pause at the top of a hill or ridge. As long as they're above you they seem to think distance a safe barrier. But deer—and other big-game animals—seem more frightened of things above them and charge frantically into cover without stopping. This deer looks as if it will do that, too.

But you'll be ready if he does stop. You scramble downhill to a little rock ledge where you slide into a sitting position. You'd like to use the sling but there's no time. And even now you find the slope too steep; you can't point downhill! The buck bounds under another rim and you can't see him anymore. Then, to your left, you hear something move.

Again, from what seems to be the air itself, a deer bounds into view. It's another deer, another mature buck. You find him in the lens and can't stay with him. He moves at a trot now, over the rocks and through a copse of aspen. On the other side he stops. His head is hidden and he must think his body is too. But you have the last ribs where your cross hairs meet, and the rifle stops wiggling in your cold hands long enough for the shot.

The deer is moving again, but out of control. You can't get the second shot but the first looked good. There's the clatter of rolling rocks, and when that stops you move ahead cautiously. Below, you spot a leg, and you know the deer is dead.

It's a fine buck but not the one you tracked all day. If you had followed the trail you abandoned, you'd have found it stayed at the same elevation, went around a point and angled up the back side of the ridge—up to where you flushed the first buck. When that buck had sensed you in the bottom he had changed direction but not destination. Instead of climbing the ridge and exposing himself to get to the next canyon, he had stayed low, working his way around the point. The fact that there had been another buck on the back side of the ridge when he got there was coincidental. It was a good thing for you, though.

So even this buck, taken with a good shot after a hard day's hunt, was as much a victim of chance as your prowess! But that's okay, because you hunted persistently and as well as you could. You made some mistakes but did several things right. You hunted several ways in two days, adapting your style to times and conditions. You played a hunch on occasion and varied your pace as you thought best. On the track, you tried to imagine where the buck was going, what he was doing and what he was thinking. You didn't follow procedures but did things that other hunters do to get a shot at a deer.

You can do those same things in the desert or on the prairie or in the wet woods hunting blacktail. You've shown how to adapt strategies to weather and terrain. Adapting to different habitat is just as easy.

Here are the techniques and tips I promised. Every one won't be important every time, but I've found them useful to know more often than not.

1. Be where you want to be in the morning 30 minutes before you can shoot. Time your hunt so you have no more than a 30-minute walk in the dark back to camp.

2. Take several compass readings in new country or when tracking.

3. Exhale through your nose to keep your breath from fogging your binoculars.

4. Hunt all day if you can hunt well all day. Time in the woods helps you get deer. Skill and time are what you have to give.

5. On days you think the hunting is poor or when you can't concentrate on your hunting, explore new territory. Hunt it, but be satisfied if all you get is a good idea of how you can hunt it again. You should always be expanding your hunting grounds, but not at the expense of prime-time hunts in familiar deer habitat.

6. Mule deer use their eyes most at long range, their ears at middle distances and their noses close up. Close up, all the senses work well. The closer you get the more careful you must be.

7. Never look a deer in the eye at short distances, even if you believe you're hidden. Staring directly at the eye of a deer looking at you will prompt him to run away.

8. Hunt with the sun to your back if at all possible.

9. Never skyline yourself on a ridge. A bush behind you is almost as effective as one in front, because it breaks up your outline. Crest out next to a bush or tree or rock or in a sharp depression—not in an open saddle. Sometimes, especially at dawn and dusk, it's a good idea not to move at all. When you sit, break

Never skyline yourself on a ridge. Crest out next to a bush, tree or rock, or in a sharp depression. If it is during dusk or dawn, try not to move. And break your silhouette with cover.

your silhouette with cover. It needn't be much, and is as effective behind you as in front.

10. Deer can see your breath in the cold, just as you can see theirs. Always try to breathe through your nostrils.

11. Deer carefully monitor those things closer than 100 yards away. Within that ring, deer perceive any threat as immediate. Their reaction depends on the cover.

12. Walk softly; mule deer have good ears and hear vibration in the ground. Wear jogging shoes where you can. Walk on trails; step over things, not on them. Be quiet.

13. You can't be silent, but you can imitate the noise of animals moving through cover. The noise you make should sound like the noise a deer makes in the places deer expect to hear deer.

14. Hunt in the rain or light snow. Gentle rain puts deer at ease, and they'll forage actively in a light rain or mist. Snow and rain confine your scent and muffle your noise.

15. When tracking, stay with one track in the snow unless you come across one as promising and definitely more recent.

16. Don't bother still-hunting in dry, crunchy conditions or on a crusted snow. It's a waste of time.

17. Stop if you make an unnatural noise still-hunting. Either wait several minutes before continuing or abandon the covert.

18. Move across wind or into the wind, but don't worry about shifty mountain breezes that blow from all directions. Worry won't change them, and even a strong prevailing wind can curl down into timber and onto the off-side of ridges, splashing scent all over. Sometimes things jutting into the wind can cause a reversal at ground level (where you are).

19. Pay attention to thermals. The deer do. Thermals start rising about 30 minutes after the sun hits the ground and they fall at night near sunset. There may be a sudden and strong wash of wind downslope at the evening shift, but in the morning thermals will rise gently. Sudden wind puffs at sunrise are not thermals, though they may be caused by temperature changes in the air. Prevailing winds cancel thermals, and there's no thermal drift on cold, overcast days.

20. Think of wind as liquid deer can taste 200 yards away.

21. Deer travel nose-to-wind when they can, but they run away from danger without initial regard to wind. When trailing deer, I often notice that I have the wind to my back. I don't know if they intentionally run with the wind so they can determine what's following them. It's a mystery.

22. Still-hunt in good cover that hasn't been disturbed with the wind in your face, as if you were stalking a deer.

23. Hunt cover that looks difficult and has lots of bushes and good escape routes. If it looks tough to you, it does to other hunters, also. The deer are likely there, avoiding all of you.

24. Assume a mature mule deer buck will hold like a whitetail in heavy cover. Hunt slowly and look.

25. Very rough or steep terrain is a poor bet unless deer have been heavily pressured. If you can walk or climb without using your hands, it's not too rugged for deer; if you have to use your hands it probably is. Deer don't like to work hard to move around; you'll find them where the terrain is easy and the plants and topography afford cover.

26. High ridges attract deer in the summer because there's little vegetation for breeding insects and there are cool breezes to keep flies away. In cool fall weather, high sunny slopes are warmer than basins that act as a thermal sink.

27. While deer generally like to see from their beds, you can find bucks on flats in tall sagebrush and in standing grain.

28. In canyon country or on the plains, look for deer at the heads of wooded draws, not down in the gut.

29. Late in the season, but before winter migrations, look for mountain deer halfway between the bottom and top where hunting pressure has been low.

30. Logging slash is a good place to find deer if it has ample leaves, needles and twigs. In winter, deer stay close to logging operations even when the saws are running. They move into the slash as soon as the loggers leave at night. The rest of the year, deer move away from active logging. Instead they forage in quiet, abandoned cuts.

31. Snow will move deer if it's deep enough to hamper movement—a foot or so. A late storm after a dry fall will move deer even if snowfall is light. Deer forage heartily before a storm, and if they migrate they migrate after it. Prolonged snowfall can prompt migration during the storm.

32. Deer will move to winter range before any snow if the snows come very late. Migration is gradual this way, unlike the mass migration after a heavy snow. Big bucks are sometimes the last to come down, but does can also stay high late in the year.

33. Look for bedded bucks in burns, on ledges with bushy cover or young trees, in thick sagebrush on hilltops and in tangles of cover on slopes. They like to bed where they can watch their

backtrail, see most approach routes and have good wind coverage.

34. When glassing, look for rectangular brown blobs, patches of off-white, shiny things and straight vertical and horizontal lines. Ears and eyes and back- and belly-lines show up most in brush; full bodies, legs and rump patches show up in the open.

35. In open country, quickly glass close, so you don't miss a deer in rifle range. Then quickly glass far away. Next, carefully glass far away, working a grid pattern. Rest often, looking for deer with your eyes unaided as you do.

36. Listen. You can hear deer move as they forage or travel or even sneak if ground litter is dry. In rut listen for the clacking of antlers as bucks spar or fight. When you hear a deer bounce, look immediately for an opening to shoot. A deer that has bounced even once is committed to run.

37. Once a deer has moved, snorted or made some other commotion deliberately, it assumes you have seen or heard it and will always move off.

38. When you see a buck, look at the antlers first and decide immediately if you want to shoot. Then concentrate only on your aiming point. If you don't have one, watch his ears and eyes and the muscles in his hams but keep the crosswires where you expect to see the shoulder or ribs.

39. In early season big bucks stay alone or in bachelor groups.

40. Mature bucks think only of themselves in escape, though bucks running together may stay together if the escape route of the buck in front is good. A mature rutting buck with a doe will split from the doe in escape, though the two will likely reunite as soon as they feel safe again. Yearling bucks follow the lead of older companion bucks or does.

41. Mature bucks run low and heavily. Young deer bounce. Stotting is more common in young deer. Listen for the clatter of brush on big antlers.

42. Mature bucks like to sneak, not run. They make better use of cover in escape than young deer and does.

43. Assume a buck will stop. Shoot while he's moving only if you have a very good position, angle and opportunity.

44. Don't shoot at a stotting deer.

45. Shoot only at a spot on the animal; know the bullet path through the deer before you shoot.

46. A deer poorly hit will head for heavy cover and water. It's best to trail slowly, after a wait of 30 minutes. The deer may stop soon, even if it's lightly wounded. But surely it will watch its back

Stotting is most common in young deer; they bounce when running. Mature bucks run low and heavy, and make better use of cover. Never shoot at a stotting deer.

trail and may hook off the trail before lying down so it can see you better. If you bump the deer once, it will be more difficult to see a second time.

47. If you don't get a shot, mark the last spot you saw the deer and its direction of travel. Try to think of its destination. If the deer is in open country and goes behind a ridge or hill you may see it again. Stalk it slowly and glass very carefully. If the deer goes into a big block of timber or tall brush you'll need snow to track and find it again.

48. If you have the track, pursue a buck as long as you can. Mule deer and blacktail can be approached again and again.

49. Run after a flushed buck if in a short distance you might be clear for a shot. If the buck stops making noise, stop until you hear him again.

50. Keep an open mind. Deer don't live by rules, and what you observe at one time may be of little use to you later. Learn as much as you can and remember what you learn. Be willing to forget what you remember if it proves useless. There are other items in my notebook. Some are elementary, but I write them down because I don't think about them enough. Other entries are blunt chidings. You probably don't need them; I deserve them and would kill more deer if I heeded them. Still others are observations about particular deer and particular country, things to remember in this drainage and reminders of the bucks that outsmarted me and how they did. That sort of thing is useful.

How It All Works

There's more to be learned from failing to kill a deer than from a successful shot. When we're successful we tend to be smug, less interested in how we could have done better.

There was the time, for instance, when I'd hunted the rubbly burn on the steep west face of a familiar ridge. I'd seen a couple of bucks, but they were yearlings. It was a hot day in early October, and by noon I was trudging along a deer trail, being noisy and going too fast. Three deer bounded out of a fir thicket above me. I didn't want the buck so I just watched them crash off downhill. Then I resumed walking.

Out onto an open rockslide I tramped without glassing, and only good fortune kept the big buck still until I could see it. He was standing above me, about 150 yards away. It had probably been with the deer I'd seen just moments before, but had split away from them and sneaked uphill. As luck would have it, I just happened to see the buck at the top of this rockslide.

I shot that deer, one of the biggest I've ever killed. My hunting partner thought that was really something, to have taken so fine a buck—and at midday. All that made me feel very accomplished, but actually the buck was doing what he should have done and I was behaving like a raw beginner, marching along the trail. I stumbled into this buck.

Not that marching is always the wrong thing to do. In fact, the beginner's luck that people talk about is often not luck at all. It's the result of beginners acting in a way that deer don't expect. The more raw the recruit, the more likely he'll bumble into a deer. The hunters who have it tough are those who behave like the deer expect them to but are not disciplined, fit or stealthy enough to see the deer first.

Doing something unorthodox in the woods is sometimes a good idea. I try new techniques all the time. But it's important to be honest with yourself. If you kill a deer while being careless, as I did on that old burn several years ago, admit it. If you've deliberately broken rules and fooled a deer that expected you to follow them, that's different. You've learned something.

Because method follows predictability, any method you use to hunt deer is fallible. Deer are predictable only to a degree, and you'll be successful only to the degree that you depend solely on method. Methods that have worked for you and for me are still worthwhile because deer will behave more or less the same this season as they did last. Still, some deer are not vulnerable to method. They have learned to predict us and have become unpredictable themselves.

5

Guns And Loads For Bear

by Richard P. Smith

Shot placement is always more important than caliber selection. A .22 Magnum rifle, for example, will bag a bear, but bullets from this small caliber don't have what it takes to do the job quickly, cleanly and consistently. Guns and loads that consistently produce a clean harvest are those that will be recommended for bear hunting in these pages.

Rifles

Many popular rifle calibers can cleanly harvest bear. Basically, any centerfire rifle .30 caliber or larger is a good choice for bagging a black bear. This general rule can be broadened just a bit to include the .270 Win., a versatile and widely used caliber for big-game hunting, and the 7mm Rem. Mag. Big bear are best hunted with cartridges in the .300 magnums and up. For brown and polar bear, the .375 H&H Mag., .416 Rem. Mag. and .475 Win. Mag. are appropriate.

Most of the black bear I've bagged with a centerfire rifle have fallen from a .30-06. In my opinion, that caliber is among the best for collecting the makings for a black-bear rug. Wayne Bosowicz, who operates black-bear hunting camps in Ontario and Maine, and whose hunters have tagged hundreds of bruins, says, "There's no match for the .30-06, period."

Leo Dollins, another veteran bear hunter and guide, often uses rifles reamed for .44 Mag. and .444 Marlin. D. DeMoss views the .358 Norma Mag. as the best rifle for big black bear, although he has also used the .350 Rem. Mag. and .45-70 Gov. with good results. Lawrence Edwards, another bear guide, has shot plenty of bear with a .30-30 Win. Additional centerfire rifle calibers that are proven black-bear getters are the .300 Sav., .300 Win. Mag., .308 Win., 8mm Rem. Mag., .32 Win. Spec., .338 Win. Mag. and .35 Rem.

There are other lighter rifle calibers such as the .243 Win. that have accounted for bear, and will probably continue to do so, but the light, fast bullets available for that caliber and others like it are not best suited to consistently penetrate layers of muscle, fat and bone to reach a bear's vitals. A hit on the shoulder blade of a bruin with a 100-grain .243 Win. bullet, for example, may break the shoulder, but stop short of the chest cavity. A 150-grain slug from a .30-06, on the other hand, will break the near shoulder, take out the lungs and probably damage the opposite shoulder just as well as if a good bullet is used.

What Is "Overgunned?"

Is it possible to be overgunned for black bear? Yes, but only if a hunter goes to such a big caliber that he or she is afraid of the recoil, resulting in flinching and poor or inconsistent accuracy. Bear are easy to kill if hit properly. The caliber rifle used will not compensate for bad hits. A poor hit is a poor hit whether made with a .458 Win. Mag. or a .30-30 Win. Hunters who wrongly believe one of the magnums is required to anchor a black bear may be more likely to make a bad hit with them than a rifle they can handle more easily, such as a .270 Win. or .308 Win.

Here's an example of how some hunters get the wrong impression about what it takes to kill a black bear. I talked with a bear hunter who was convinced that a .30-06 was not adequate for black bear after his first successful bear hunt in Nova Scotia. He did bag an average-sized bear on the hunt with an ought-six. However, the bruin went about 100 yards after the shot before dropping. He admitted the hit wasn't the best (missing the lungs and heart), but for some reason thought it was the rifle's fault.

As a result, he returned the following year with a rifle reamed for .460 Wthby. Mag. Fortunately, he practiced with the rifle, becoming proficient with it. He eventually got a shot at a bear, and hit it in the chest. It dropped on the spot. He was pleased with the big bore, but failed to realize a .30-06 would have put that bruin down just as quickly with the same hit.

Being "overgunned" for black-bear hunting is possible, but only if the chosen caliber's recoil is too much for the hunter to handle. Black bears are large animals; they require a good first hit.

Bullets

I've used both 180- and 150-grain soft nose bullets in my .30-06 and have gotten the best results with 150s. The heavier bullets sometimes go completely through the bruin without expanding inside. The slightly faster 150s expand more and are often found just under the skin on the side opposite entry, expending all of their energy inside the carcass. Put another way, I've flattened more black bears in their tracks with 150-grain bullets than 180-grain bullets, and would recommend their use in any caliber.

In calibers that cannot use 150-grain (or a similar-weight) bullets, heavier bullets will have to suffice. For example, bullets for .44 Mags. are available only in 240-grain size. However, there are two bullet styles available: soft point and semi-jacketed hollow point. Soft points are the better choice because hollow-point bullets sometimes mushroom too fast, preventing complete penetration.

There's more to rifle selection for bear hunting than caliber. How much a rifle weighs, sights and its type of action are important factors, too. The primary hunting method you use will dictate, to some extent, what choices to make. If you will be hunting with hounds, for example, you will want a light, fast handling rifle that will be easy to carry. (It's not unusual to follow hounds for miles over rugged terrain covered with thick brush.) A sling makes carrying a rifle easier on these types of hunts and will leave your hands free to handle the dogs. Keep this in mind when selecting a rifle for this type of hunting.

Sights

Iron sights are adequate for most hound hunts, but telescopic sights are a good choice for stand hunting, plus spotting and stalking. Scopes are invaluable for their light gathering ability early and late in the day. Plus they magnify and ease aiming at medium to long ranges. Some shots at bruins feeding on grass during the spring in Western states and Canada can be at hundreds of yards, while most shots when watching baited sites are 75 yards or less. Either fixed or low power variable scopes such as 1½-5X are fine for stand hunting where shots are expected to be 100 yards or less, while the 2½-8X or 3-9X power variables are better suited for use in areas where shots can be longer.

Other Considerations

Rifle weight isn't as important when stand or still-hunting and stalking as it is when chasing after hounds. Bolt-action rifles are generally more accurate than other actions, and will be most beneficial when hunting openings. Beyond that, rifle actions are a matter of choice.

Flat shooting rifles such as the .270 Win., .30-06, .308 Win., 7mm Rem. Mag. and .300 Win. Mag. are good all-around rifles for any type of black-bear hunting; however, they are especially good for medium- to long-range shots possible while spotting and stalking. Other rifle calibers such as the .30-30 Win., .32 Win. Spec., .35 Rem., .44 Rem. Mag. and .45-70 Gov. work best for close shooting, when hunting with hounds or over bait.

Muzzleloaders

Black powder rifles in .50 caliber and larger are recommended for hunting black bear. Percussion cap models are better than flintlocks because it's easier to keep the powder dry, and when taking a shot the powder charge ignites instantly. With flintlocks there is a split second delay between hammerfall and discharge. (The rifle must be held on target to ensure accuracy.)

Two bruins have fallen to my Thompson/Center .50 caliber Hawken. Fellow outdoor writer Dave Richey also killed a black bear with a similar muzzleloader while hunting with me. All three black powder bear were shot with 370-grain maxi-balls propelled by 100 grains of FFG powder. Two of the bruins ran 50 yards before piling up. The third dropped on the spot.

A number of percussion cap muzzleloaders, like the Knight MK-85, are designed to shoot modern rifle bullets with sabots (pronounced say-bos), a type of plastic patch, in addition to round balls and maxi-balls or bullets. Hornady sells boxes of bullets complete with sabots for use in these rifles. Jacketed hollow-point .44 caliber bullets are available for use in .50 caliber front loaders and jacketed flat point .44 caliber bullets can be obtained for use out of .54 caliber MK-85s.

Today's muzzleloaders have one other major feature that sets them apart from replica front loading rifles. They have double safeties that dramatically reduce the chances of an accidental discharge. The nipple is also recessed in an action that is similar to a bolt-action rifle's, reducing the chances that moisture will affect firing of caps or powder charge.

Projectiles

Although we used bullet-shaped maxi-balls made by Thomp-

NAHC Life Member David Hofius took this fine grizzly with his .54 percussion rifle. The bear had a 27-inch skull and measured 9½ feet.

son/Center to bag our bear, round balls should also do the job. Ballistically, round balls are faster and have more energy than maxis. We decided to use maxis because of their greater weight. Round balls for .50 caliber muskets weigh 175 grains.

Maxi-balls propelled by 100 grains of FFG black powder have a muzzle velocity of 1,418 feet per second and 1,652 foot-pounds of energy, according to a Thompson/Center booklet. Round balls with the same powder charge leave the muzzle at 2,052 feet per second and have ballistics comparable to the .45-70 Gov. and round balls come closest to the .44 Mag.

Hornady makes a "Great Plains" maxi-bullet that should also prove effective. These bullets have hollow bases compared to the maxi-ball's flat base. They come lubricated, too. Great Plains .50 caliber bullets are available in both solid and hollow-point designs. Hollow points weigh 385 grains and solid points weigh 410.

Powder

Most muzzleloaders come with owner's manuals that list the best loads to use for hunting. However, as a rule of thumb, the amount of powder to use for big-game hunting loads can be determined by multiplying the caliber by two. For .50 calibers then, a good load would be 100 grains and for .54 calibers, 108 grains (actually 110 grains for ease of measuring).

Some owner's manuals suggest optimum powder charges for target shooting rather than hunting. Based on my experience, 90 grains of powder should be the minimum charge used for bear hunting with a .50 caliber front loader and 100 grains should be a minimum for a .54 caliber. Lighter charges often do not produce enough velocity for projectiles to pass through bruins, which is important in yielding a blood trail to follow should a bear run off after the shot. Be sure to test various loads in your rifle to determine which produces the best accuracy and trajectory.

Residue from burned black powder builds up inside the barrels of a muzzleloader after several shots, making it increasingly difficult to load. For this reason, it is a good idea to bring a cleaning rod and patches to the range in order to swab the barrel between shots.

There are several types of black powder that vary in size of individual granules. FG powder has the coarsest granules and is generally used in shotguns. FFFG has fine granules and is often used to charge handguns and prime the pan of flintlocks. FFG powder is in-between and is generally recommended for use in rifles. Pyrodex, a modern version of black powder, is also popular among front loading rifle users.

Patches

No patch is required between powder and maxi-balls or bullets. Lubricant is added directly to maxi-balls and a ramrod is used to seat them on top of the powder. When using round balls, patches are required, either lubricated cloth patches or plastic cup-shaped patches made by Butler Creek Corporation in Jackson Hole, Wyoming. I've used both and have had more consistent groups with plastic patches. However, test them yourself to determine which works best in your rifle.

Other Accessories

It's necessary to carry plenty of accessories when hunting with a muzzleloader. Besides powder and maxi or lead balls and patches, you will need a powder measure, a ballstarter to start round balls or maxis down the barrel, plus percussion caps or flints, depending upon the type of muzzleloader used. If using a percussion cap model you will also want to carry a nipple wrench and an extra nipple. Leather pouches, called possibles bags, are often used to carry these accessories, but a couple of big pockets will also work.

To speed up reloading I generally carry two or three pre-measured charges of powder with me. I used to put each charge in empty, plastic 35mm film containers and lubricated maxi balls in other containers. Now I use double-ended plastic tubes with caps on each end to serve the same purpose. The powder charge goes in one end and the maxi or lead ball and patch in the other.

Shotguns

What about shotguns for hunting black bear? Using a 12-gauge is okay for shooting slugs. But if you have a choice between using a shotgun and a rifle of one of the calibers recommended earlier, use the rifle. Generally speaking, buckshot should not be used for black-bear hunting. Buckshot does the job sometimes, usually at close range, and at others, fails. Because buckshot does not produce consistent results I do not recommend its use.

I was with a friend of mine who shot his first black bear with a 12-gauge shotgun. Jim had a slug in the chamber and 00 buckshot in the magazine for backup. A bruin gave him a perfect chest shot at 20 yards when it stood up on its hind legs to reach bait in a tree, and Jim made a good hit. However, the bear dropped on all fours and rather than going down, ran away. Jim hit the bruin twice with buckshot as it ran. The bear only went 50 yards before piling up.

The slug had done the only damage, hitting the lungs. The buckshot that was recovered didn't make it through the bruin's heavy layer of fat. Buckshot loads have been improved since then, but I still think they are a poor choice for bear hunting. Hunters who decide to hunt black bears with a 12-gauge shotgun and slugs should use a slug barrel with iron sights or a mounted scope, for accuracy.

Handguns

Hunters serious about bagging a bear with a revolver have three proven choices—the .41 Rem. Mag., .44 Rem. Mag. and the .454 Casull. The .357 Mag. will kill black bear, but it's not a bear gun. Either soft or hollow-point bullets can be used for black-bear hunting with handguns. Bullets ranging from 210 grains to more than 300 grains can be used in these revolvers. Of course, in single-shot pistols like the T/C contender and Remington XP-100, traditional rifle cartridges like the .45-70 Gov. or the .350 Rem. Mag. can be used.

Many hound hunters elect to carry handguns instead of rifles

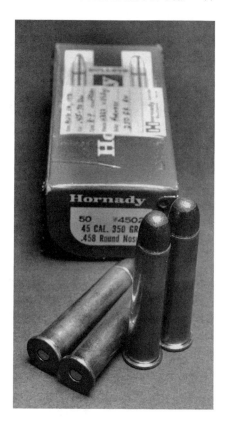

One pistol cartridge that is commonly used when hunting big bear is the .45-70. The bullet that is shown here is a Nosler 350-grain roundnose.

for a number of reasons. Sidearms are lighter and easier to carry than long guns when following dogs. When holstered, a hunter's hands are free to handle hounds. And more importantly, handguns are easier to handle than rifles when in the middle of a bear and dog fight. At close quarters, which often exists in such a situation, a handgun is more maneuverable than a rifle to put a bullet in a bear without endangering dogs.

The area of big-game hunting with handguns was revolutionized with the advent of single-shot models such as Thompson/Center's Contender that handles cartridges formerly reserved for rifles. Contenders are available with 10- and 14-inch, interchangeable barrels in a number of calibers suitable for black-bear hunting. The .30-30 Win. with 150-grain bullets is a prime example. Rick Powell shot a black bear with a Thompson/Center Contender in that caliber one fall. The bear was treed by Lawrence Edwards' hounds. Other calibers to choose from are the .35 Rem., .41 Rem.

Mag. and .44 Rem. Mag. Faster velocities and more energy are obtained with the same bullets from 14-inch barrels than from 10-inch barrels.

One of the best calibers in single-shot handguns for black-bear hunting is not available from Thompson/Center, but barrels can be custom made by J.D. Jones from SSK Industries. The caliber is the .375 JDJ, named after Jones. Cartridges are handloaded from .444 Marlin brass with 220-grain, soft-nose bullets.

If you are considering using a .45 Colt handgun for black bear, you might be better off leaving it at home. A fellow hunting with some friends of mine shot a treed bruin with a .45 Colt. None of the slugs penetrated into the bruin's body cavity. The bullets spent all of their energy plowing through hide and fat. That 200-pound bear was killed with a .44 Rem. Mag. handgun when the .45 Colt proved ineffective.

Well, there you have it. Solid recommendations for choosing centerfire rifles, muzzleloaders, shotguns and handguns, plus their best loads. If you follow these recommendations and place your shots properly, you shouldn't have trouble bagging a bear.

6

Bows And Broadheads For Bear

by Richard P. Smith

Selecting a bow for bear hunting is not as simple as it used to be. I'm not referring to the draw weight though. That's still easy. What makes bow selection difficult today is that there are so many designs from which to choose. When I started bowhunting, bow styles were limited to recurves and long bows, with recurves being the more popular. Since then the compound bow has taken over in popularity. There are still archers hunting with recurves, and there has been a resurgence in the use of long bows following the same trend as gun hunters turning to muzzleloaders from their popular centerfire rifles.

Bows with a draw weight of at least 50 pounds are generally accepted as minimum tackle for bow hunting black bear. That should be considered an absolute minimum, and hunting archers should strive to work up to the 70-pound area for bear, especially the big-bear species.

Comfort and accuracy are the two key considerations when selecting a bow. It is always a poor choice to sacrifice accuracy and comfort for speed and power with a bow. If you have to strain to pull a bow back to full draw on the practice range, you may not be able to draw it at all when a bear walks into view and you become tense, excited, nervous and anxious all at once. Shot placement is more important than power and speed when it comes to bagging a bear, whatever the hunting tool.

Long Bows

Long bows represent the simplest and oldest form of bowhunting equipment, with long limbs that have a slight or gradual curve in them. These bows are appropriately named because they are usually more than 70 inches long; many measure 76 to 78 inches. Long bows of this length are required to propel hunting arrows at desirable speeds of 170 to 185 feet per second.

Recurves

Recurve bows use shorter limbs to achieve faster arrow speeds of up to 190 feet per second. Limbs of recurves bend inward at sharper angles than long bows, then curve outward near their tips. Recurve bows vary in length from 50 to 68 inches. Longer recurves shoot faster arrows and are smoother in the draw and release than shorter models, making them more desirable for hunting. Sixty inches is a good average length for recurve bows used for hunting, with those a little longer probably being better choices than bows four or five inches shorter.

My favorite recurve measures 60 inches in length and has a 52-pound draw weight. The bow was made by the American Archery Company in Wisconsin. I claimed three black bears with that bow before switching to a compound.

Takedowns

Recurve bows are available in takedown as well as one-piece models. Takedown bows have distinct advantages over one-piece recurves or compounds if you intend to hunt with hounds. Takedowns can be strapped to a packframe, leaving hands free to fend off brush, climb slopes or handle dogs before, during and after the hunt.

Long and recurve bows can and should be unstrung at the end of the day, as well as when transporting by airplane, in vehicles and on horseback. In some instances hunters carry the strung bow by hand when on horseback.

The more simple design of recurve and long bows reduces the chances that something will go wrong with them. Limbs can, however, be twisted if they aren't strung and unstrung properly. For this reason, a bow stringer should always be used for stringing and unstringing stick bows.

Compounds

Pulley operated compound bows that combine cables with the string increase arrow speed, producing flatter arrow trajectories.

The following six photos are from a 35mm sequence camera showing Fred Bear arrowing a brown-bear trophy with bow and arrow on the Alaskan Peninsula in May 1962. Above: Fred and his guide, Ed Bilderback, are hidden behind a rock as the bear approaches along water's edge.

And that isn't all. Compounds make it possible to shoot heavy draw weights while only holding a fraction of that weight—40 to 65 percent—at full draw. By comparison, long bows and recurves become progressively harder to pull back the farther they are drawn, with maximum force exerted on fingers at full draw. This makes it quite difficult to hold heavy hunting bows of either recurve or long design at full draw without getting shaky and making a sloppy release.

Compounds, on the other hand, are hardest to draw when the arrow is only partway back to your anchor point. When the string is pulled far enough so the pulleys "roll over" the holding weight drops off or relaxes a certain percentage, depending upon the bow used and the number of pulleys it has. The difference between draw weight and holding weight of most two wheel compounds is 50 percent, but some are available with as much as 65 percent letoff.

Here, the brown bear continues along the beach. Fred's arrow is ready to be drawn at any second.

The big bear changes his course, sees the hunters and looks them over a few seconds from 20 feet. Fred has his 65-pound Kodiak bow at nearly full draw.

The bear ignores the hunters. With his bow fully drawn, Fred waits until the bear's front leg is forward. That way, he can place the arrow behind it and enter the most vital area.

Fred releases the arrow and it strikes the bear. The arrow is buried to the feathers. The bear roars in rage and leaves in high gear.

The distance of the shot was 20 feet. The arrow penetrated completely and punched through the skin on the off-side. The bear ran 90 yards.

Another advantage some compounds have over recurves and long bows is they are available in adjustable draw weights, usually in 10- to 15-pound increments. Beginning bowhunters can purchase compounds with various pound draw weights: 50 to 60, 45 to 60, or 60 to 70. They may elect to start shooting at the lighter draw weight for target practice, eventually working up to maximum weight for hunting. Compounds average shorter in overall length then recurves, but are generally heavier due to the materials used in their construction.

Cams And Overdraws. Cams and overdraws are modifications to compounds that increase arrow speed. Replace round pulleys with programmed cams and the result is faster, flatter shooting and more powerful bow. The only other difference is that bow with cams, rather than round wheels, are often a little harder to draw. The string has to be pulled farther back before the bow "breaks" or relaxes in draw weight. This is something that is easy to get used

Fred Bear with his brown bear that squared 9 feet. Its skull measurement was 27 inches, and it weighed 810 pounds. The razorhead arrow had done the job well. The bear lived less than 30 seconds after the arrow hit.

to with practice, though. I've bear hunted with a cam bow, the PSE Vector, for a number of years. When I first got the bow I had difficulty drawing it at 60 pounds, being used to a 50-pound round wheel compound. However, after a couple of weeks of drawing the bow around the house several times a day my muscles adjusted to the added strain.

Overdraw bows are compounds modified to shoot shorter, lighter arrows. Arrow rests are moved back behind the sight window to accommodate shorter arrows. Light arrows fly faster than heavy ones, producing flatter trajectories. However, because of the arrow's light weight smooth releases are a must. For this reason, most bowhunters who have overdraw bows use release aids instead of gripping the bowstring with fingers.

Some hunters think overdraws have shown that penetration on big game is not exclusively dependent on arrow weight. For many years the majority of bowhunters have favored heavy arrows to achieve maximum penetration on big-game animals. Arrow penetration on big game with shafts released from overdraw bows has been terrific, suggesting that arrow weight isn't the only factor affecting penetration. Arrow speed is probably important, too, along with other factors.

Tom Nelson at Anderson Archery in Grand Ledge, Michigan, says a friend of his consistently gets 254 feet per second with 25-inch 2013 shafts out of his overdraw bow. Tom says his friend's bow is set at 70 pounds. Before modifying his bow for overdraw use, this bowhunter was shooting 31-inch, 2219 shafts at 210 feet per second.

For comparison, Tom says that cam bows shoot arrows at 220 to 230 feet per second, while round wheel compounds average 200 feet per second. It should be understood, however, that arrow speed varies tremendously from one bow to the next, even among the same make and model. Another maxim to remember is that arrow speed alone will not harvest a bear. Arrow placement and sharp broadheads combined with sufficient arrow speed will drop a game animal. Fast arrows and flat trajectories are a lot more important bowhunting considerations when pursuing mule deer, antelope and caribou—those species that require longer shots at unknown distances.

Accessories

With the exception of long bows, most modern bows are designed to accommodate sights and accessories such as stabilizers, string trackers and more. Nonetheless, if you plan on using these items, or others like them, be sure the bow you choose for bear hunting has places for them.

If at all possible, obtain a bow for hunting that is camouflaged at the factory. Otherwise, you will have to camouflage shiny limbs yourself. Camo tape is handy for doing so, or spray paint can be used. The job doesn't have to be fancy. The objective is simply to dull the bow's finish and reduce its visibility to game when you are in the woods.

Recommendations

All of the bow designs discussed are satisfactory for bear hunting within the draw weight suggestions mentioned at the outset. However, I would recommend round wheel or cam compounds for most bowhunters for bagging a black bear. After taking half a dozen bears with my PSE cam bow, I switched back to a round wheel compound set at 60 pounds. The Bear Super Magnum 44 I'm now using draws smoother and is easier to hold at full draw, and it still gives me plenty of arrow speed. I prefer a 60-pound draw weight over a 50-pound draw for bear hunting because it increases the chances for complete arrow penetration on bruins. The presence of entry and exit holes increases the chances of having a good blood trail to follow.

If you are a traditionalist and like to keep your equipment simple, long or recurve bows are good choices. Steer clear of stick bows with fiberglass limbs. Instead, select recurves and long bows made of layers of wood and glass, with glass as the outer layer. Long bows are suited for bowhunters with good instinctive shooting ability, although there's nothing that says you have to put a sight on a recurve or compound either. Recurves are slightly better for bear hunting than long bows because they are shorter and easier to handle in thick cover where bears are often found; they also throw a slightly faster arrow.

Hunters interested in more arrow speed than available from cam bows and who are willing to use a release aid, should select an overdraw bow. Most bow manufacturers have overdraw bows on the market, or at least kits that can be used to convert conventional compounds to overdraw capability.

Hunters who get a compound and don't know how to tune it themselves should have someone knowledgeable do it for them. A compound that is out of tune is difficult to shoot properly. While you are at it, have the draw weight checked to be sure it is accurate. The actual draw weight of a bow is sometimes different than what its label says.

Draw Length

Hunters need to know their draw length to select the proper bow and arrows of the appropriate length. An easy way to determine draw length is to hold the end of a yardstick on the center of the chest so it parallels the ground. Reach out toward the end of it as far as possible with both arms. The measurement at the tip of fingers is the draw length.

Arrows

It is important to shoot arrows matched to a bow. This is why hunters should know the actual draw weight of their bow. Fortunately, arrow manufacturers make it fairly easy to make the right arrow selection. Some companies have an arrow selection

When bowhunting big bear, experts recommend using a bow weighing 60 pounds with 500-grain arrows. This will help maximize penetration. Bears, such as this huge grizzly, have heavy hair and many fat layers making penetration difficult.

chart for aluminum shafts that clearly shows what shaft sizes to choose for stick and compound bows in respect to draw weight. The weight of broadheads you will use is also important when determining which arrows to use and this variable is also shown in the chart.

I hunt with a compound set at 60 pounds and shoot 4-blade Bear Bruin broadheads weighing 145 grains. My draw length is 28 inches, but I hunt with 29-inch shafts to allow for clearance of heads. According to the arrow selection chart, I could use five different shaft sizes, with 2314s and 2216s the most commonly used. However, 2117s fly well out of my bow and are one of the five choices. That is the shaft size I shoot.

If I were hunting with a 60-pound pull recurve, the recommended shaft sizes, according to the chart, are 2315, 2219, 2413 and 2512. Most stores that specialize in archery equipment have these selection charts available and can tell you which size shafts will perform best out of your bow based on your draw weight, length and choice of broadheads.

Draw weights of long and recurve bows are based on a 28-inch draw length. Long and recurve hunters who shoot arrows less than 28 inches in length should subtract three pounds draw weight for every inch less than 28; they should add three pounds draw weight for every inch the bow is drawn beyond 28 inches.

Aluminum shafts are the choice of most serious bowhunters because they are light and strong, plus they are usually closely matched from one shaft to another in the same size. Shafts are also made from cedar and carbon. Some wooden arrows have a tendency to warp, but are often the preferred shaft material among traditional bowhunters. Cedar arrows should not be used with compound bows.

AFC is one of the major manufacturers of carbon arrow shafts and they have arrow selection charts to help hunters choose the correct size shafts. Their chart shows that 2200 shafts would be the best choice for use with my 60-pound compound. Arrows in size 2400 are recommended for hunters shooting 60-pound recurves.

Carbon shafts are slimmer than those made of aluminum, so hunters who will be switching to them may need a new quiver or may have to adapt the one they have to hold carbon arrows.

Fletching

Arrows are fletched with plastic vanes or feathers. Vanes are waterproof; feathers aren't. However, feathers can be waterproofed somewhat by covering them with hair spray or a spray made specifically for waterproofing purposes. Feathers can be shot off arrow shelves and vanes can't. Vanes require the use of an arrow rest. Feathers are also more forgiving of a poor release than vanes, but are noisy if bumped or brushed against anything. The choice between the two is simply a matter of what shoots best with your particular setup.

Broadheads

There are a lot of different broadheads to choose from, many of which are adequate for bear hunting. The two basic types of broadheads available today are those that require sharpening before use and those with presharpened, replaceable blades.

Popular choices in the former category are Bear Super Razorheads, Zwickey Black Diamond Deltas or Eskimos, and Rothhaar Snuffers. Bear heads have two main blades and they are designed for the addition of razorblade inserts to give them four blades. The Zwickey Deltas and Eskimos are available in either two- or four-blade models, with the Deltas being the larger of the two. Snuffers are large, heavy three-bladed heads that should only be used with bows pulling 60 pounds or more due to their size.

Examples of broadheads with presharpened blades that have proven themselves on bear are Bears, Rocky Mountains, Savoras, Brute Fours and Razorback 4s and 5s. As the names imply, Razorbacks are available in either four- or five-blade models, and Brute Fours have four blades. Rocky Mountains and Savoras come in three- and four-blade models. Bear makes a wide variety of replaceable blade heads that have either two, three or four blades.

Small, two-bladed broadheads are required for use with overdraw bows. Tom Nelson said Zwickey Eskimos and Satellites are used by some bowhunters with overdraw bows. The Hunter's Edge is another small head that works with overdraw bows.

The Bear Razorhead has bagged most of my bow-killed bear. Recently I switched to their 4-blade Bruin. Even though the Super Razorheads are supposed to be ready right from the package, a touchup is often required to make them razor sharp. Hunters who aren't willing to take the time to sharpen heads like the Razorhead, Delta and Snuffer should use presharpened models.

There are a variety of sharpening tools available on the market to aid in effectively sharpening broadheads. Most bowhunters use a file and/or whetstone to put smooth, sharp edges on their heads. The key to putting the best edge on broadheads is to maintain the same angle between the sharpening tool and the edge as it is being sharpened. I've had excellent success sharpening broadheads with a Razor Edge kit.

The importance of using sharp broadheads for bear hunting with bow and arrow cannot be overemphasized. I've mentioned proper shot placement with both rifle and bow in an effort to emphasize the extreme importance of this final step in shooting a bear. For a bowhunter, razor sharp broadheads are a must!

7

Trailing A Wounded Bear

by Richard P. Smith

Most bruins bagged with bow and arrow disappear from sight before expiring, and some shot with firearms do the same. The purpose of this chapter is to provide helpful information on how to follow and locate these animals. If shots are placed properly, the hunter will be trailing a dead bear. However, there will always be situations in which animals are not killed due to a hunter's error or to circumstances beyond his or her control, and a wounded black bear must be tracked down and finished.

Shot Placement

Many hunters may not realize it, but the most important aspect of trailing wounded bear comes as the shot is taken. The factor that determines how easy or difficult a trailing job will be and how far a black bear will have to be trailed is shot placement. This may sound familiar by now. It certainly should. If I accomplish nothing else here other than to impress upon readers the importance of only taking high percentage shots at bruins, I'll be happy.

Part of the problem is that many bear hunters are already successful deer hunters and they assume shots that put deer down will work on black bear. This is true to some extent, but not in every case. One major difference between deer and bear is the size and position of the lungs. Most black bear have smaller lungs that are positioned farther forward in the chest cavity.

Before going on a black-bear hunt, hunters should become familiar with where to place their shots. When you're aiming a loaded rifle at a live bear it is not the time to start learning bear anatomy.

String Trackers

Bowhunters can do one more thing to prepare for a tracking job by obtaining and using a string tracker. In most cases, these tracking aids enable bowhunters to follow arrowed bruins even if there is no blood, and I highly recommend them. The reason is that black bear do not bleed as freely as deer, and sometimes leave no blood trail for the first 50 to 100 yards. The layers of fat on a black bear's body (especially during the fall) and their long-haired hides retard blood flow.

There are a number of string trackers on the market, but the best one I've found for bear hunting is a Game Tracker. This tracker is available with either white or orange line in 17- or 30-pound test. The heavier line is best for bear hunting, and white line is easier to follow at night.

The tracker line is fastened to the forward end of the arrow shaft by holding it in place between the back of the screw-in broadhead and the shaft. The line should be taped to the end of the shaft for added insurance on the chance the head unscrews as a bear runs. Arrow trajectory isn't affected out to about 30 yards on bows of at least 50-pound pull, which is well within the range of most bow shots at black bear. However, hunters should test the devices before hunting with them to make sure they work properly.

If using a string tracker with small capacity spools of line, be sure to hunt with a full spool or one that is almost full. A bowhunter who was bear hunting with me one year was using a model containing a small spool of orange line. He had taken several practice shots with the spool he hunted with, leaving little line on the spool. When the guy took a shot at a nice bear the remaining line balled up and was too large to feed through the opening in the container. The arrow had enough force to snap the line and went on to hit the bear. However, the arrow used so much energy breaking the line that there was insufficient penetration to yield a one-shot kill.

String trackers are not infallible. Sometimes the line breaks soon after a bear is hit, or the arrow may pull out and the line comes with it. But when they do work properly and the line proves helpful in locating a bear, they are worth their weight in gold. This

String trackers have become a virtual necessity for bowhunters. They help increase the odds of locating downed black bear quickly.

Keep your wits about you when you're following a wounded bear. Pay attention to details and check ahead carefully before you proceed.

potential advantage outweighs the disadvantages by a long shot. They prove valuable even on missed shots by enabling bowhunters to locate their arrows quickly and easily. And when a bear is arrowed, hunters need not worry about finding their way back to where they started from. The string will lead them to their trophy and back to their stand.

I used a Game Tracker when I connected on my black bear in Colorado while hunting with guide Jim Jarvis. The device worked perfectly, feeding line out with the running bear for the 50 to 75 yards it covered before piling up. My arrow passed completely through the bear leaving a double line to follow. The line went from my bow through the bear and to my arrow, which was embedded in a tree trunk at the bait.

Hunters who use string trackers must accept the responsibility for picking up used string at the end of a hunt. Failure to do so leaves an eyesore, and might lead someone to your bait station.

After The Shot

Bear hunters who familiarize themselves with proper shot placement, taking only shots they should, and bowhunters who use string trackers are a step ahead of those who don't when it comes to trailing a bruin they have hit. The procedure to follow immediately after a hit varies, depending upon whether a firearm or bow and arrow was used. As a general rule, gun hunters should follow up shots immediately and aggressively with another shot, with the exception of those using single-shot firearms such as muzzleloaders. Bowhunters should be passive, waiting before taking up the bear's trail.

With A Firearm

Gun hunters should be ready to put a second slug into a bear after the initial shot, and should do so if the animal shows any sign of life. If the animal drops, rolls or runs out of sight after being hit, move up to the point where it was last seen as quickly as possible or at least to a spot where the bear is once again visible, and use a second bullet if the animal is not yet dead.

Hunters using firearms will have to rely upon their ears to determine the next course of action when bear are out of sight upon reaching the point where the animals were standing when shot. Listen carefully for any sound such as crashing brush, coughing or moaning that may give away a bruin's location or line of travel. Visually and mentally mark the location of any telltale sound by picking out a distinctive feature such as a nearby tree for reference.

If there is a lot of commotion in one location, the bear is probably down, but not yet dead. Proceed to that spot quickly and finish the animal. As black bear die, they sometimes moan loudly when air is expelled from their lungs. The sound isn't pleasant, and has sent chills up the spine of more than one novice black-bear hunter; however, hunters who know what it means can proceed directly to the spot where the sound came from to claim their kill. Lung-shot bruins will sometimes make coughing or gurgling sounds as they expire.

Sounds of a running bear may also be heard. Black bear usually crash through branches and brush on a dead run when shot, making lots of noise. Mark the spot where the last sounds are heard. The animal either dropped at that point, slowed to a walk, reached an opening or stopped to lie down. If you are sure of a good hit and that the animal is probably dead, you can move to the spot where the animal was last heard to find the carcass. Hunters who are unsure of the hit or uncomfortable about following a bear alone should make sure the spots where the bear was hit and last heard are carefully marked, then go for help.

When returning to recover the bear, make sure you have something with you to mark a blood trail, such as tissue, surveyor's tape, or a spool of Game Tracker line. This line is the best choice, in my opinion, because the line leaves a continuous trail rather than a broken one to refer back to when looking ahead for new blood sign and can be followed out more easily once done tracking. There are 2,500 feet of line on a spool of 17-pound test. This is one way that gun hunters can make use of archery equipment. If it is dark, or will be soon, bring flashlights with fresh batteries or a lantern to help in locating a bear. Under these circumstances, leave guns and bows in the vehicle. It is illegal to have either in the woods after shooting hours end.

If a dead bear is not located where the animal was last heard, search the surrounding area for sign. Blood will have exited both sides of the animal if the bullet went through, but only on the side of entry if it didn't. A running bear often leaves noticeable scuff marks on the ground where it lands between strides, if not clearly defined tracks. Freshly broken branches, bent or broken saplings, turned leaves, crushed logs and damaged stumps may be other sign of the wounded animal.

Mark the bear's trail once it has been located, then move ahead, marking each additional track or spot of blood, unless there is a steady flow that is easy to follow. Frothy blood is a sure sign of a lung hit and a short blood trail. Bright red blood may mean a heart shot or arterial wound. Dark red blood usually originates from the liver. Intestinal matter mixed with blood is an indication of a gut-shot. If the bear is hit in the evening and the weather permits, trailing of a gut-shot bear should be resumed first thing the following morning. If it's hit in the morning, you should wait at least four hours.

In situations where the bear's course of travel can't be located in the vicinity where it was last heard, return to where it was hit and try to work the trail out from there, circling back-and-forth across the bruin's probable path until locating blood. There should at least be hair at the spot where the bear stood when hit, and blood is often present, too. Follow blood trails as far as possible, keeping noise to a minimum to avoid scaring the bear off if it is still alive, and also to hear the animal if it should move. If trailing during hours of daylight and a bear is jumped, try to shoot the bear again

Trailing a wounded bear in dense cover, this hunter switched to a shotgun loaded with slugs. It's a tough combination to beat at short range.

to finish it. If it stays too far ahead, wait several hours or until the next day to resume trailing.

A bruin that's hit with a bullet and goes one-quarter mile or more without lying down is probably not seriously hurt. One that is properly hit usually won't go that far. Nonfatal injuries may leave plenty of blood initially then gradually taper off to nothing. A poor blood trail may not be an indication of a poor hit, though. Most bleeding on a hit high in the body will be internal, so don't give up too soon.

Under circumstances where no blood can be located or the blood trail ends after a short distance, hunters must do their best to relocate the trail or find the animal by covering as much ground as possible. Crisscross the terrain in the direction the animal was headed until it is covered thoroughly. When they have a choice, wounded bear often travel downhill and may go to water, but not always. Keep this in mind when coming to a dead end on a blood trail. If there are clearly defined trails where the blood stops, follow these as far as possible for further clues.

Using A Dog

The absolute best way to find a bear when there is little or no blood to follow is to rely on a hound. One that will follow bear scent doesn't need blood to determine where a bear went. I've used a hound on a leash as an ace in the hole to locate downed bear for years and have recovered some that would have been impossible to find any other way. My dogs have also made it possible to determine that bear not found were healthy enough to recover from their wounds. This is because you can follow the animal much farther with the help from a dog than by blood sign alone.

I feel very strongly that all serious black-bear hunters should own at least one hound for trailing purposes. In states and provinces where hunting with hounds is not permitted, allowances can be made for tracking dogs restrained on a leash, provided the hunter first notifies and gets permission from the game warden. Most wardens will probably permit the practice, but hunters must inquire ahead of time to protect themselves. Wardens may want to go along, or at least be notified each time a dog is used to trail a bear. Always do your research before planning a trip.

When trailing a wounded black bear with a hound, proceed as you otherwise would. If the animal is still alive and jumps, mark the location and return later. In the morning, hounds with good noses can follow a bear scent which was left the previous evening.

If a good dog is available, use him! Well-trained dogs take the guess work out of locating wounded black bear.

The two dogs I've used for this purpose have done so. If more than one bear dog is available when a bear is jumped and if hunting with hounds is legal, then both hounds can be released in an effort to bay or tree the bear. A single dog stands a better chance of being hurt or killed by an injured bruin than two or three, but sometimes one hound can successfully tree or bay a wounded bear.

One fall I brought my Plott hound, Charlie, along to help trail a bruin that had been hit with a broadhead. The animal was shot at a bait in the evening and we took up the trail the following morning. There was plenty of blood to follow initially, but when we eventually jumped the animal where it had bedded for the night, the bleeding had stopped. I was convinced there was no way we would catch the bear with the dog on a leash because the bruin was healthy enough to move out ahead of us without us hearing or seeing it, so I let Charlie go on the bear's trail.

The dog was in good shape and I figured he would be able to stay out of the bear's way long enough for us to catch up and finish it, if the bruin stayed on the ground. As it turned out, the bear treed after about a half-mile chase and was finished with a firearm. There is no way that bear could have been trailed and harvested successfully. As it turned out, the arrow wound wasn't fatal. If it weren't for Charlie, I'm sure that bear would have recovered from the injury.

On another occasion, a fellow I was guiding shot a bear with a .44 Mag. caliber rifle during the morning and was unable to find the animal. I put Drew, a black band tan, on the trail several hours later. The dog led me toward a steep, rocky hillside several times, but I didn't think an injured bear would climb it, so I kept stopping the dog short and went back to the bait to start over again. Eventually, I let the old hound have his way. He went right back to that hillside. There was the bear, hiding among the rocks.

There were a number of downed trees on the hillside, too, and when we got close to where the bear was hiding, Drew lunged ahead and jerked me into one of the trees where I fell and lost my grip on the dog's leash. The hound ran ahead and I got back on my feet just in time to see the bear run downhill ahead of him. I took one shot at the bruin, but missed. Drew bayed the injured bear at the bottom of the hill behind some big boulders.

I hobbled toward the action, having injured a knee, only to hear my dog start to move off before reaching the bottom of the hill. When I rounded the last boulder and saw what was happening I discovered the tables had been turned. The bear was chasing

Approach a downed bear with extreme caution. Move in from the rear, then work around to the head and check the eyes for reaction.

Drew at that point and the dog's leash was dragging on the ground. If the leash hung up on branch, the hound would be in trouble.

My next shot had to count, and it did, but I don't even remember aiming. When I shot, the bear dropped with a broken shoulder and I pumped two more rounds into him to make sure. Drew's chances of being hurt were increased because of the leash, but even without such a handicap a single hound may be hurt by a wounded bear.

On that particular day I was carrying a 12-gauge shotgun and slugs. Since then I started carrying a .44 Mag. handgun, freeing both hands to handle the dog.

All of the wounded bear I've jumped, with or without a dog, day or night, have run away. However, it always pays to be cautious. Wounded bear that are cornered have been known to turn on their pursuers, both hunters and hounds. If a bear did attack when being trailed with a hound, it would make sense to release the dog to distract it. When trailing without a dog, always keep an eye out ahead and to the sides in an effort to avoid close contact with a bear that may still be alive.

Hunters who have access to a bear dog and hit a bear they are unable to trail shouldn't wait too long before putting the hound into service, especially if other bear are in the area. The presence of bear scent fresher than that from the wounded animal may distract a hound, reducing its effectiveness in following the right animal. Scent fades, too, with time. Rain and wind accelerate the process. Even under favorable conditions, trailing a bear with a dog should be started within 12 hours, but only if permission to do so has been granted by the game warden. If I'm having trouble with a blood trail, I try to put a dog in action within three to four hours so the scent is as fresh as possible.

If more than 12 hours elapse before a dog can be put on the trail of a wounded bear, or if the blood trail has been washed out, all is not lost. If a bruin is down within a reasonable distance of where it was shot, a hound can locate the carcass by winding it. A dog worked into the wind to check for the animal will sometimes find it.

The first black bear I shot with a black powder rifle didn't leave a drop of blood, although I was sure I connected. I aimed for the bruin's chest as it sat facing me. Since I was hunting close to home, I got Drew and we were on the bear's trail in about an hour. The bear had only gone about 50 yards before expiring. My maxi-ball hit a little lower than aimed, but still did a good job. The reason there was no blood was the slug didn't exit and the hole of entry was plugged.

I probably would have found that bear without the dog, but it would have taken longer, and there was a chance the carcass would have gone undetected. The animal went down in extremely thick cover in a swamp. With the dog, there was no question I was going to locate the bear, as I did. Any bear hunter can up his odds of finding bear he hit in the same way.

Any type of bear dog can trail a wounded bruin. Hounds that are on the small side such as females are best suited because they are easier to handle on a leash.

Charlie was Drew's replacement and the Plott hound weighed in around 80 pounds. Charlie was sometimes hard to control on a hot trail because of his size.

Not all hounds take to a blood trail willingly, so a little training is helpful. Take the dog on the trail of a number of bear that you may have already located or ones that leave an easy-to-follow blood trail. Then praise and reward the hound once the carcass is reached.

Whenever the carcass of a black bear is located always approach from the rear and look for signs of breathing. Also look at the eyes. The eyelids are always open on a dead bear. If they are closed, the animal is probably still alive and should be shot again. Whether the eyes are open or closed, every downed bear should be approached with extreme caution.

Hunters using single-shot firearms should reload as quickly as possible, then follow the same procedures for trailing bear outlined above. The reloading process for front loading rifles can take minutes to complete, so hunters using them may want to listen to determine what course a bear takes, if it does run off, before starting to reload.

With A Bow And Arrow

In most cases, a black bear hit with a broadhead runs off so fast there is no time for a second shot. However, on occasion, a second shot is possible, and bowhunters should be ready to take advantage of the opportunity. Fellow bowhunter Dave Bigelow hit one of the first bear he tagged with two shafts, dropping it in sight. When hit with the first arrow, the animal spun around in a circle, giving Dave enough time to nock a second arrow and put it in the bear's boiler room.

Michigan bear hunter and taxidermist Jim Havemand, from

Traverse City, once grazed a nice boar with his first arrow and it ran a short distance then stopped, giving him a 10-yard broadside shot. Havemand's second broadhead sliced through one of the animal's lungs, redeeming the bowhunter.

When a bear is arrowed, bowhunters should try to see where the shaft hits. Although this is not always possible, the knowledge can be useful in deciding how long to wait before beginning tracking. Bright fletching, especially orange and yellow, show up well against a bruin's black fur and can help you judge shot placement. Solid chest/lung hits will kill quickly. Hunters should wait at least an hour after a liver hit; the liver is located in the middle of a bear's body. At least four hours should elapse before following a gut-shot bear.

Archers using string trackers will get an idea of how good a hit they made by watching how the line pays out, provided the device works properly. If line uncoils rapidly for a number of seconds then stops and moves again, but at a much slower pace before stopping for good, that's a good sign. It's not a good sign if the line keeps unraveling until the spool is gone. In situations where the animal is still heard running and the line has stopped moving, the arrow either pulled out or the line broke. Under those circumstances, hunters should mark the location where the departing bear was last heard.

Bowhunters not using string trackers should note at what point a bear goes out of sight, the direction of travel the animal is taking and the location where the bruin is last heard. The bowhunter should remain completely quiet for at least five minutes to look and listen for any further clues to where the bear may have gone. Then, the bowhunter should wait for an additional 15 minutes. If he hears no new sounds, he should leave the area as quietly as possible. It is important to be quiet on the chance the bear is bedded nearby. Any disturbance may cause it to get up and move off, making the recovery process more difficult.

An exception to the wait-in-place philosophy when a black bear is arrowed is when the animal is paralyzed from a spine shot, but still alive. Try to get another arrow into the animal from your blind or stand; however, if the animal starts dragging itself off (and this is possible) carefully go after it to put an arrow into its lungs immediately. But keep your distance! A black bear with only the use of its front quarters can still cover ground in a hurry. And he won't be in the mood to chitchat. Lawrence Edwards guided a hunter one fall who hit a bruin this way and didn't attempt to finish

Good trailing techniques produced a quick recovery on this black bear for NAHC Publisher Mark LaBarbera.

the animal. It was hours later before the guide arrived and they followed blood to where the bear stopped to rest. From that point on there was no blood and the bruin was lost. The paralysis was apparently temporary, the rest giving the animal an opportunity to recover.

Once an appropriate amount of time has elapsed (20 minutes for a heart/lung shot, four hours for a gut shot), return to the spot where the bear was hit and begin trailing the animal by following the string or blood trail. If your tracking string begins to move, the bear may still be alive. The best thing to do is back off for an hour or more before starting after the bruin again.

Since both firearms and archery equipment are legal during most, but not all, bear seasons, bowhunters can often have a partner carrying a gun accompany them when tracking—provided it's during legal shooting hours. My brother Bruce was my backup when trailing the first couple of black bear I shot with bow and arrow. A gun is most useful if a bear is still alive and a follow-up shot with a bow is not possible.

Under these circumstances, it is the hunter's responsibility to finish the bear as quickly as possible with a bullet. Hunters who insist on pursuing a wounded bear with a bow when the odds of getting a decent shot are against them are unethical and unsportsmanlike. They are more concerned about their ego than the quarry and the sport. The chances of recovering wounded black bear are reduced by relying solely on bow and arrow.

If hunting during a bow-only season, the hunter has little choice and must try to finish the job with archery equipment, unless a game warden or conservation officer can be contacted and is willing to assist with a firearm or give the bowhunter permission to use a gun. When night trailing, hunters must leave guns and bows behind, of course. The best course of action to follow when a bow-shot bear is jumped, whether day or night, is to mark the area carefully so it can be located again and quietly back off, waiting a number of hours before returning. The animal probably won't go far if pursuit is broken off right away.

Blood Trailing

In situations where there isn't much blood, hunters can sometimes see better by getting down on hands and knees. Rust spots and red pigment on leaves can sometimes be mistaken for blood. Blood spots that have dried wipe off easily with a wet finger. Rust and red pigment won't. Crushed berries sometimes leave blood-like stains on vegetation, too, so be aware of it and try not to be led astray by these possible distractions.

Three people are ideal for following a blood trail. One person carefully scouts for sign, another marks the sign and remains on the last clue until another is located. The third person keeps a watchful eye on the surroundings. When only two people are present, one searches for new clues while the other remains at the last clue and watches the surroundings. If more than three people are on hand to follow a wounded bear, one person should take charge to conduct an organized search. Too many hunters, some who may not know what to look for, can trample blood sign or tracks before they are recognized.

Bowhunters who have made good hits should find their bear within 200 to 300 yards, but keep trailing as far as possible until the bruin is either located or you are convinced it wasn't seriously hurt. Even minor wounds may yield a long blood trail, but

When blood trailing your wounded bear, it is ideal to have three people. One scouts for sign, another marks sign and the third watches the surroundings. It is also nice to have some help when it comes to field dressing the animal after it's found.

bleeding may be heavy at first then taper off or be sparse the entire time. Bow hits can sometimes be difficult to judge based on blood sign. Arrows that sometimes look like they go into the chest cavity slide along the outside of the ribs, especially on shots at bear angling away from a hunter at an extreme angle. In most cases, the lungs were missed if a bear goes beyond 200 or 300 yards; but, the bear can still be found.

There are several reasons why I feel it is important to locate bear as soon as possible after they are shot, which sometimes results in trailing them during hours of darkness. There's always the chance of rain, and sometimes snow, to wash out a blood trial.

Dead bear that are left in the woods overnight may be eaten by other bear or wolves. I've only had this happen once, but Wayne Bosowicz reports that it has happened a number of times to kills made by his hunters. In some cases, the entire carcass has been devoured.

In addition, the longer a bear carcass sits without removing the viscera and allowing the meat to cool, the greater the chances of spoilage of both meat and hide. Heavy bear hides hold heat in, resulting in extremely fast spoilage in warm weather. If handled properly, bear meat is excellent eating, and hides are great trophies. Both are worth preserving.

8

Guide Your Own Elk Hunt

by Dwight Schuh

Dreaming about roaming the high, wild, and lonesome on your own, footloose and free as a mountain man is one thing. It's another to place yourself in the realities of mountain life and come out with the same self-respect and enthusiasm you started with. Most elk country, and the elk themselves, can disillusion you quickly if you're not prepared.

Why is elk hunting tough? Mike Lapinski, who is one of the co-authors of the NAHC's Hunter's Information Series book, *All About Elk*, has guided elk hunters in Montana and has also helped nonresidents plan their own elk hunts. One year he helped three experienced hunters from Wisconsin plan a bowhunt for elk during the bugling season. These hunters had all taken several deer and bear apiece, so they were hardly novices, yet they came away from their elk hunt discouraged.

One obstacle that exceeded their greatest imagination was the physical demands of Western hunting. Even though they all had been running and lifting weights to prepare, they found their conditioning woefully inadequate. In talking to other hunters, particularly those from the East who have never hunted big mountains at high elevations, I found that reaction to be widespread.

Lapinski's friends also had difficulty adapting to the nature of the elk themselves. They had read extensively about elk, but they still didn't understand their habits, and they had a tough time

Many novice elk hunters underestimate the physical demands. If you can't handle prolonged exertion in steep terrain, the self-guided hunt may not be for you.

locating animals. And when they did find bugling bulls, they didn't know what to do with them. Elk hunting bore few similarities to the deer and bear hunting they had perfected back home. The average hunting success in Montana is about 15 percent, but one of the Wisconsin hunters, after his initial elk expedition, said he would give the beginner on his own a zero to one percent chance of success.

I believe your chances are better than that, but the experience of those hunters does point out one important fact: The self-guided elk hunt is not for everyone. You must be a special breed of cat to make it work.

Test Yourself

How do you know if you're the man or woman to take on elk hunting by yourself? To answer that question, examine yourself. Some hunters have the ability to fare for themselves and other don't, and there's no sense in kidding yourself. Evaluate your own abilities honestly.

First, how dear are time and money to you? If you're short on time and long on money, planning your own hunt is probably counterproductive. Self-planning takes time, and if you don't have time to spare, hiring an outfitter could be cheaper.

Outfitted hunts are often viewed as expensive undertakings; however, but when you consider the horses, transportation, camping gear, and other expenses attendant to any serious elk hunt, you discover that outfitting yourself isn't cheap. If you plan to hunt elk every year, the expense may be justified, but if you'll hunt elk only once or twice in your lifetime, the money you would pour into equipment would be largely wasted.

Physical ability plays a big part, too. Hunting on your own requires considerable physical demands in setting up your equipment, hiking miles on foot, handling your own game and cooking for yourself after a long day in the field. If you're a vigorous person who thrives on exertion, then you'll probably do well on your own; however, if that's not appealing, then you'll fare better with an outfitter who will supply a horse for you to ride, butcher and pack your game, have meals prepared at night and other niceties on such a trip.

Planning your own elk hunt takes a certain amount of initiative and research, and to do that you must be a self-starter, the kind of person who thrives on doing things for himself. If you're easily discouraged or frustrated when things go awry, you'll have a hard time on your own as an elk hunter. On the other hand, if you thrive on challenge and can turn defeats into victories, then you're probably cut out for self-guided elk hunting.

You don't have to have experience with elk to hunt these animals successfully; a fundamental knowledge of woodcraft, outdoor lore and wildlife is essential. If you know your way around the woods, know how to read sign, spot animals and stalk, have done some game calling and so forth, then you probably can adapt quickly to Western conditions and can hunt elk well. But if you've had little hunting experience and plan to take on elk as your first quarry, do it with an outfitter who has the needed lore.

Define Your Goals

Once you decide you're qualified to hunt on your own, the dreaming ends and the planning begins. Research is the secret word. If you do your homework, odds are you'll have a great trip. If you simply head to the mountains on a prayer, hoping things will work out, chances are overwhelming that Murphy's Law will get the best of you.

Before you can do any meaningful research, you have to know what you expect from a hunt. Business efficiency counselors advise, "You can't get somewhere unless you know where you're going. So set some goals." If that's true for businessmen, it's equally true for hunters. You must know what you want before you can plan for it.

First, what kind of an elk are you looking for? Will you settle for nothing less than a 6-point bull? Will any bull regardless of size satisfy you? Would you be happy shooting any kind of elk, including a cow?

Do you insist on an area with lots of elk, or would you settle for fewer elk as long as you can enjoy some solitude and beautiful scenery? Do you want to bugle a bull, or would you prefer to track him in snow? Do you want to backpack, horse camp or car camp? Are you looking for easy access or wilderness?

Brainstorm with your hunting partners and write down all your ideas. Keep at it until you've built a composite picture of the ideal hunt. Now you've got some basis for further planning.

Hunting Modes

Buying Your Own Horses. In the minds of many hunters, elk and wilderness go together. Long-distance wilderness hunting, say more than five miles from the road, requires horses or other pack

Some hunters who go after elk every year find it worthwhile to buy their own horses. You can keep them at home and trailer them to your hunting area, or you can board them with a local rancher.

animals. Some hunters who hunt elk yearly find buying their own horses worthwhile. Many keep their horses at home and trailer them to the hunting area, but others find it simpler and probably cheaper to pasture their horses with a rancher near the hunting area. The use of horses for back-country hunting is a specialized subject beyond the scope of this chapter, but it's a workable alternative if you plan to hunt elk seriously.

The Drop Camp. For most hunters, this may be the best all-around option for self-guided wilderness hunting. You either can hire an outfitter to set up a camp for you, using his equipment and gear, or you can have him drop off your own camping gear at a predetermined location.

Even drop-camp hunts demand planning. If you rely strictly on a packer to choose the location, you could find yourself in a bad spot. He may have a number of drop camps, and you could find yourself in a crowd even in the wilderness. Or if the outfitter is running guided hunts at the same time, he may stick you in a second-rate location. Obviously, he'll take his guided hunters into the prime country. For these reasons, you're wise to pick your own location (I'll detail research methods later) and to tell the packer where you want your camp.

In addition, make sure services are clearly outlined. A friend of mine arranged a drop camp. The outfitter agreed to set up tents and tables and provide stoves, lanterns, gas and other needed accessories. When my friend arrived in camp, 17 miles from the nearest road, he found no white gas. He spent several days in the dark, cooking over a campfire.

In another case, I killed a deer early in a hunt. The outfitter, as prearranged, showed up at the end of the first week to pack out the meat. He promised to place the deer in cold storage. When we emerged from the backcountry at the end of two weeks, I found my deer still hanging at air temperature at the outfitter's base camp, the meat molding badly.

In another situation, an outfitter quoted me a price of $100 to pack out an elk. After I had killed a bull, the price suddenly jumped to $400. Naturally I about exploded. The outfitter patiently explained that he had been talking about a different area. My elk was in a rough spot, much farther from the road than he had anticipated, so he had to charge me more. Make sure before you ever set out that the details of a hunt are clearly understood by both parties.

Backpacking. Regardless of the hunting mode, you'll pay dearly for a backcountry hunt. To hire a packer you pay in money; to backpack you pay in energy. My friend Larry Jones, during a week-long backpack hunt in Montana, well expressed the reaction you may feel in backpacking for elk.

"Why do we do stuff like this? Why don't we just hunt off the road like everyone else?" Larry groaned as we slumped to the ground to relieve our bodies from the burden of heavy packs.

"Maybe we're crazy," I replied.

"Maybe, nothing," Larry sighed.

That's probably not an atypical reaction among backpacking elk hunters. Sometimes it hardly seems worth the effort. On the other hand, backpacking gives you excellent mobility, and the achievement of doing it all yourself offers satisfaction that few other forms of hunting can match. I've backpacked for elk many times in rugged terrain for periods lasting as long as two weeks, and I've enjoyed some excellent hunting while doing it.

Backpacking is an inexpensive way to hunt elk, but quarters are cramped and the amount of gear you can take with you is limited.

However, backpacking has its limitations. If you envision saddling yourself up with two weeks' provisions and roaming 20 miles from the nearest road, and then packing out a bull elk on your back, you're dreaming. The amount of food and gear needed for two weeks, particularly during cold weather, will weigh 80 to 90 pounds, and a bull elk will require about five trips at 100 pounds each. You had better invite Superman along on your hunt if you plan to tackle that chore.

Realistically you have to gear a backpack trip to your own strength and endurance. For me, backpacking has been ideal for hunting as far as three to five miles from the road for up to a week at a stretch. This kind of hunting allows me to hunt farther off-road than the average day hunter will venture, but the rigors of the trip don't destroy me physically. Before you set out on a back-packing adventure, do some backpacking at home to find out what you're made of and what you can endure. Then in planning your hunt, choose an area that's compatible with your abilities.

Hunting from Roads. Don't assume you must hunt wilderness to find elk. You may face more competition from other hunters near roads, but 75 percent or more of the elk hunting today exists in road-accessible areas. You'll find plenty of elk there. Hunting in Oregon, I hiked 200 yards off a paved road next to a logging operation and immediately walked into a herd of elk. Backup beepers on logging equipment were making so much noise nearby I scarcely could hear the herd bull bugling, but I still pulled him within bow range. In Arizona, a friend said he used the noise of cars passing on a nearby highway to cover up his sounds as he stalked a bull. The point is, elk are where you find them, and that isn't always 20 miles beyond nowhere.

The car-camper actually has an advantage over backcountry hunters. In the wilderness, mobility is limited. With a drop camp, for example, you're tied to a central location; in backpacking your range is limited by time and energy.

In contrast, by car you can travel roads freely to explore new areas, and you can radiate out much farther from camp than if you're stuck in a central wilderness camp. You also can drop buddies off at the top of a ridge to hunt down to a road below and use your vehicles in other ways to save yourself time and energy.

Hunting by road, you have several options. One is to stay in a motel. In some cases that will work; however, realistically, most good elk country contains few motels, and hunting out of a motel will require an excessive amount of driving to and from the hunting area each day.

Some hunters tow camp trailers or small tent trailers into elk country. For early-season hunting, when roads generally are in good shape, that's a fine option, but a trailer does limit flexibility. You can't negotiate rough, backcountry roads with a large trailer, and even if you do, especially during October and November, you face the potential for getting stranded by heavy snow or rains.

A preferable option is to set up a large camp in a central location. Most serious elk hunters own several large canvas wall tents, each with a wood stove, and they erect elaborate tent towns for their annual elk trek. That's a practical arrangement for late-season hunting because it gives you a comfortable home where you can warm up and dry clothing after a cold, wet day in the field. A reliable, warm camp is essential for enjoyable elk hunting.

For early-season hunting (August and September) when shelter and warmth are not so critical, you can camp out of your truck, which allows you the greatest mobility. In many cases, successful elk hunting requires finding an area where undisturbed animals have concentrated. Camping out of your truck, you can hunt an area one day, and if it doesn't pan out you can throw your gear into the vehicle and head to another spot immediately. You can keep moving until you find an ideal location.

One commonly asked question is: How long should I plan to hunt? Finding elk can take time, and if this is your first hunt, you'll spend a few days just learning an area. I personally wouldn't plan for less than 10 days, and I feel more comfortable with two weeks.

Research

A personal contact may be your most valuable aid in planning a hunt. A person who knows the country and the animals can teach you more in one hour than you can learn in years on your own. If you don't have personal acquaintances in the West, contact game

You must have warmth and comfort to enjoy the rigors of an elk hunt, especially during the late season. A large base camp comprised of quality wall tents suits many hunters' needs.

departments, Forest Service offices, sportsmen's clubs or other groups to strike up a friendship. Even if no one can hunt with you, someone may take time to point you in the right direction when you arrive to hunt. The North American Hunting Club opens up many opportunities along this line, and chances are you can swap an elk hunt for an interesting trip in your local area.

Equally good would be to take a guided hunt your first time around. In the long run it could save you many dollars. One Minnesota hunter hired a guide his first year in Idaho, and then he returned on his own and killed elk the next two years. In contrast, I've talked to hunters who've tried on their own for several years and have never seen an elk. It's a lot cheaper to hire a guide one year to learn the ropes than to spend four or five frustrating, elkless years on your own.

If you can't find a personal contact and refuse to hire a guide, you'll have to plan your own hunt from the ground up. That may seem like a prodigious task, but if you passed the test at the beginning of this chapter, you've probably got what it takes. Just don't skimp on the research. Hunters who complain about a bad experience generally set out half-cocked; those who make it on their own usually research and investigate extensively. The value of research can't be overemphasized.

Selecting an area can take time, and you can expect to run up some phone and postage bills, but the time and expense will be worthwhile. In most cases the quality of your hunt can be directly related to the extent of your research. Over the past years, I've planned many hunts to new areas. A few have bombed, but consistently when I've done my homework the hunts have far exceeded my expectations.

Remember one thing about hunt planning: It's not an exact science. Below I've listed the general steps; however, this is not a precise prescription for a guaranteed hunt. Your success depends a lot upon your ingenuity. But by applying some of these guidelines, you can assemble a composite picture of conditions that should lead you to a good hunt.

Picking A State. Many hunters arbitrarily pick one state because a friend hunted there or they read about it in a magazine. I think that's a mistake, as one example points out. A fellow from Arkansas wrote and said he had problems hunting the San Juan Mountains of Colorado because he had heart trouble and the elevation there was too high. His doctor told him to hunt at lower elevation, and he wanted to know of such a spot in Colorado.

Apparently he assumed Colorado was the only state worth hunting for elk. In reply I told him to hunt elsewhere. The lowest point in Colorado is 3,800 feet, and in elk country the lowest elevations are closer to 7,000 feet. In most places you hunt from 9,000 to 11,000 feet. My advice was to hunt in Idaho, Montana or Oregon where elk live in lower country.

Unless you have good reason to hunt one particular state, begin your research by ordering big-game regulations from all Western elk states. (If you want to hunt on your own, forget about Alberta and British Columbia—unless you live there—because these provinces require nonresidents to hunt with guides). Studying all the regulations is the only way to get an overview, and you must know the range of possibilities before you can make a wise choice.

Some states, for example, offer six-week bow seasons and a month-long rifle season. Others have split seasons that fall in either October or November. Some states have seasons only in October or November. Some states have seasons only in October, and others have seasons during the rut. Some states do not have rut-hunting seasons for rifle hunters, but they do for bowhunters. Check for restrictions on the number of hunters, and see whether the state offers limited-permit "trophy" areas or special antlerless licenses. And, of course, look at the license and tag fees. Also, if you want to plan a combination hunt, say for deer and elk, examine the regulations for this potential. In some states combination hunts are possible, and in others they're not.

When you send for regulations, ask for harvest statistics as well. Don't be misled by sheer numbers. For example, in Colorado the total elk kill is close to 30,000 and average hunter success is 17 percent. In Arizona the total kill is less than 2,000 elk, but rifle-hunting success ranges close to 35 percent, and the average bull is much larger than in Colorado. At the same time, read everything you can get your hands on about different states and regions. At the library, the *Readers Guide to Periodical Literature* lists hunting articles in outdoors magazines by state, so you can get some good ideas there.

Read books, too. Many of Jack O'Connor's writings take you on adventures in the West's famous elk regions. The Boone and Crockett and Pope and Young record books serve as definitive directories to trophy hunting. Reading also may give you further sources of information—people that you can talk to for more specific details.

In addition, utilize the wealth of taped material available these

Audio and video tapes can be quite an asset when planning your self-guided elk hunt. Most sporting goods stores carry these types of cassettes.

days. Dozens of companies produce video and audio cassette tapes, many of which take you right along on actual hunts, and some are hunting movies. Also, some companies provide information on how to use your equipment, such as maps and compasses. Tapes and movies are no substitute for first-hand knowledge, but they can give you a feel for the experience. A friend of mine bought a couple of tapes on elk bugling from Wilderness Sound Productions of Springfield, Oregon. He listened to the tapes continually. By the time he went hunting he felt like a veteran elk hunter, and on his first hunt he enjoyed thrilling action from day one. Few tapes give you a concrete idea of where to hunt, but they can familiarize you with the overall elk hunting experience so you can avoid some surprises.

Maps. Once you've settled on a state or two, order public land maps—most will be National Forest maps—for the entire state. Also order state topographic maps from the U.S. Geological Survey. A map is little more than an aerial picture of the country, and it provides you with a view of prospective hunting country right from your living room. From maps you can determine the elevations involved, general topography, the nature of drainages, the road systems, accessibility, the proximity of towns, facilities, campgrounds and many other necessary aspects of a hunting trip. Eventually, different areas will begin to stand out in your mind. Note these areas and begin to make a list of questions, which will serve as the basis for further research.

Personal Contacts. Next to actual scouting, locals who know the territory and the conditions are your best sources for information.What you're looking for is experience. If you lack it, the next best thing is somebody else's. Plan to contact hunters, biologists, foresters and other sources by telephone. The person who won't spend five minutes writing a letter will talk for an hour on the phone.

A couple of general guidelines apply to all phone research. First, ask specific questions. If you simply call a person and say, "Can you tell me the best place to hunt in Colorado?" your answer will be something like, "Well, the whole state has good hunting." Then you're no better off than when you started. Besides, general questions promote vague answers. However, if you call up and ask something like, "I've noticed that Bear Creek has no roads into it, and game department figures show good hunting success there. Can you tell me what the country looks like in Bear Creek, and why the hunting success is high there?" In response to a question like that, a person either must say, "I'm not telling," (and if he says that, the place is probably worth investigating further), or he has to give you a specific, useful answer. As you interview people over the phone, have a complete list of questions at hand, and keep maps of the areas discussed in front of you for quick reference.

The other reason to do some research ahead of time is to gain the confidence and trust of those that you are interviewing. Hunters call me frequently to get information. If someone obviously has done no homework and is simply looking for a free lunch, I'm evasive. On the other hand, when somebody demonstrates that he has researched on his own and is on the right track, I find myself opening up, probably because I'm willing to help someone who has tried to help himself. Sometimes I even reveal secrets I should keep quiet.

Here's one final guideline: Double-check your findings. Never take the word of just one source. I try to contact three sources on each prospective area. If one person tells me an area is excellent hunting for big bulls, I then call another source, and then another. If they all say, "Yeah, man, that place is full of big bulls," then chances are it's true. But if their responses contradict each other, I'm skeptical and dig further before committing myself.

Big-game biologists may be the most valuable sources because they work with animals year-round, and as public servants most are fairly free with their information. However, some biologists aren't hunters and they view game herds differently from the way a hunter would, so don't stop with biologists. From your reading try to get the names of hunters in the area. You can probably make contacts through sporting goods stores or local newspaper writers. Also contact Forest Service and BLM offices and talk to resource people there. They spend plenty of time in the field and often will share their observations.

Your line of questioning will vary, depending upon your goals and your findings from previous research, but some topics apply to most hunt planning. Below I've listed topics I always try to address, and this list may help you scout by phone.

Biology Of The Area. This has to do with the quality and quantity of elk. If you simply want to kill an elk, regardless of size, look for areas with the highest elk densities. One clue is total harvest. Units with the highest harvest probably have the most elk. In parts of northeast Oregon, for example, big bulls are scarce, but elk are numerous and chances for killing a small bull or cow are excellent. The same applies to the famous White River country in Colorado. Elk densities are high so your chances of seeing animals are good, but because hunting pressure is high, few bulls live long enough there to reach trophy status.

If you simply want to kill a meat animal, consider applying for a tag in one of the many limited-permit antlerless hunts. Most states offer cow tags, and these tags are most commonly issued in areas with excessive numbers of animals.

To assess the number of animals in a given region, ask biologists how they would rate densities in certain drainages—low, medium, or high? Hunters or loggers probably won't think in terms of densities, so ask something like: How many elk live in the Black Creek Drainage? One? Five? 10? If I hunt there during the rut, how many bulls could I reasonably expect to hear bugling during a day of hard hunting? Two? 15?

If you want a trophy bull, say a mature 6-point or larger, the criteria differ. One starting point is the Boone and Crockett record book. It points out those areas where some of the largest bulls have been taken. From this you can discern which counties or national forests have produced trophy animals.

Another way to determine the trophy quality of an area is the bull-cow ratio. In high-production areas with a high elk harvest, the bull-cow ratio may be as low as 5 to 10 bulls per 100 cows. In other areas where hunters are limited for one reason or another, the bull-cow ratio may be as high as 30 to 40 bulls per 100 cows. The greater the percentage of mature bulls in the herd, the better your chances for taking a trophy animal. Most authorities agree that the post-season ratio should be 20 per 100 or higher for good trophy hunting. In some cases, you can get figures that show bull-cow ratios, but it takes some digging. It's easier to ask local biologists: Which drainages have the highest bull-cow ratios? Why is that true?

In any good trophy area, hunting pressure is limited in some way. In many cases, it's a function of natural conditions. Inaccessibility may be one, and that's why the percentage of mature bulls generally is higher in deep wilderness than in well-roaded areas.

However, don't be fooled into thinking wilderness holds the only good bulls. In many cases a true wilderness, such as the Bob Marshall Wilderness Area in Montana or the Selway-Bitterroot in Idaho, gets hunted more heavily than some more accessible regions. That's because the general rifle season runs for two months in many Wilderness Areas, and outfitters hunt there intensively for the full two months. For that reason, fringe country with small roadless blocks scattered among accessible drainages often has better trophy potential than deep wilderness. Few outfitters operate in such country, and there's enough backcountry to provide good sanctuary for elk.

Terrain and vegetation may also serve as natural sanctuary for trophy bulls. In parts of northern Idaho and Montana, the jungle-like brush and trees provide elk with good refuge cover in well-roaded country, so trophy bulls survive even amid intense hunting pressure. In southwest Colorado, some rugged canyons will make you dizzy just looking up at them. If you've got the grit to hunt such places, you can find trophy bulls within a quarter-mile of paved highways. Ask local sources about the potential for such sanctuary areas. It seems like every region has its notorious "Hell Hole" or "Black Canyon" where nobody in his right mind would shoot an elk. If you're after a trophy, that's the place for you.

Finally, don't overlook man-imposed sanctuaries. Many states restrict the number of hunters in certain units to promote quality hunting. Colorado has designated several units as trophy areas; Utah has some limited-entry hunts that produce huge bulls; all hunting in Arizona is limited entry; Oregon has "3-point or better" units that maintain high numbers of bulls. In most cases, limited-entry systems yield higher hunting success than general seasons, and the bulls generally are bigger. Inquire about the quality of limited-entry hunts.

Access. Along a similar vein, you want to determine access. Your maps show roads; however, from that you can't necessarily determine the quality of the roads, especially under varied weather conditions and you can't determine the current status. Logging, mining and other development continually open up new roads, so all maps are necessarily out-of-date even before you get them. Many states have imposed road-closure systems, some only during the hunting seasons and others permanently. Therefore, roads shown on your maps may not be open to travel. Also, many old maps show trails that no longer exist, and in other cases have been turned into jeep roads. During your research, ask about the present condition of the road systems and trails, and update your maps to avoid time-wasting surprises when you start hunting.

Terrain And Vegetation. Elk country varies infinitely. In the higher ranges of Colorado and Wyoming, you find classic elk country—timberline basins and alpine meadows, pockets of black timber, frigid springs bubbling from the ground. In parts of Colorado and Utah, however, elk thrive in nasty canyons with oakbrush and aspens. In northwest Montana, elk country consists of steep, low-elevation mountains blanketed with mile upon mile of endless timber. In Arizona and New Mexico, major herds thrive on pinion-juniper flats that look more suited to lizards. In other words, there is no such thing as "typical" elk country. You want to start out with a valid picture in your mind, so ask local sources: What kinds of trees are these shown on my maps? Is there heavy underbrush, or is visibility good? Do tight contour lines shown on my maps represent cliffs, or simply steep hills? By asking such questions, you can gain a clear picture of the country.

Movement And Habits Of The Animals. In some regions, elk are primarily grazers, and in other regions, where meadows are scarce, they browse on leafy plants. Ask locals what the primary forage plants are, and at which elevations you can expect to find most elk. In some country, they'll stick to a narrow elevational band right at timberline; in other places, they're scattered throughout forested slopes.

Also, ask about movements and migration patterns. In some parts of the Southwest, elk live year-round in one small locality. In mountainous, high-elevation country, they may move up and down

Elk terrain can vary considerably. In some states, elk can be found on timberline basins and alpine meadows; in others they can be in canyons or low-elevation mountains. Elk are considered to be grazers; however, they do eat leafy plants occasionally.

considerable distances depending upon immediate conditions. An early frost can force animals from the high country down into the lower river drainages where the feed remains green. A heavy snowstorm could push them from one drainage into another. During a wet year, they may congregate around certain meadows, but following a dry summer, when those meadows dry up, the elk may move into heavy timber or other well-watered areas to seek lush feed. Ask locals what elk would do under various conditions. That way, if you don't find animals in one kind of habitat or at one elevation, you'll know where to continue the search.

Livestock. Some areas are heavily grazed by sheep and cattle, and I've found it frustrating trying to hunt elk among herds of cattle and sprawling bands of sheep. Find out if livestock roam the same ranges you plan to hunt, and if they'll be moved out by the time the hunting season opens.

Campsites And Water. In many areas, water is no problem because springs and creeks are numerous; in other regions, water may be scarce and you may have to bring your own. In some places you can camp about anywhere, but in other regions camp spots are at a premium. Get some suggestions on prospective campsites before you set out.

Weather. Weather will influence your camp gear and clothing selection. During August and September, you would expect warm, balmy weather, and you'll probably get some like that, but you're just as likely to get snow. Later in the season, you can expect blizzards and deep snow and temperatures down around zero. Always ask about the weather and determine what would be the worst type of weather you could anticipate and prepare for it accordingly.

Scouting

The final planning step, once you arrive at your prospective hunting area, is scouting. Before you start, it's important to understand the nature of elk. If you've hunted nothing but deer, you might have trouble adapting to elk and their unique habits. First, remember that elk are herd animals, and they'll range in small bands from two to three animals up to a dozen or more. Unlike deer, which may be scattered evenly throughout a mountain range, elk herds will live in specific pockets, and the territory between herds may be elkless.

Habitat To Look For. Elk are heavy-bodied animals with very thick coats, so particularly during the early fall, you'll find them

Be sure to check out the availability of water for your camp needs; it comes in handy for cooking and drinking. In some places it's plentiful, in others you'll have to bring your own.

primarily on north and northeast slopes where temperatures are coolest and vegetation is thickest.

Elk hang out around wet meadows and spring seeps where moisture cools the air and where they can wallow in the mud. The heads of drainage basins and low points where springs ooze from the ground are good locations. Elk are primarily grazing animals, so any area that has lush, grassy meadows and parklands adjacent to heavy cover for bedding and refuge may attract elk. In some regions, grass feed is scarce, and the elk will feed on alder trees, huckleberries and other leafy browse. As you scout you want to look for these cool haunts with good feed.

Topographic features often serve as a guide for locating elk. High alpine basins with grass on the higher slopes and heavy timber for bedding at the lower ends often attract animals. Most elk country is very steep, so animals will frequently bed on small, flat benches.

Hunting pressure, especially during rifle seasons, can influence the location of elk. As you scout, try to pick out pockets of heavy vegetation or roadless drainages where the elk can find refuge from hunters.

Scouting Methods. Before you start hunting, it's essential to have an overview of your country. Try to arrive a couple of days before the season so you can look around before you start hunting. Even if you arrive during the season, you're smart to spend a couple of days looking before you even consider hunting. Unless you have a personal contact to show you where to camp and where to hunt, I suggest that you not set a permanent camp until you've scouted and have decided where to hunt.

One way to get a quick overview is to hire a local pilot to fly you over the country for an hour or two. An aerial view can save you many hours of scouting on the ground.

If that's not possible, pick out vantage points. Fire towers present the best views; however, any high mountain, bluff or ridgetop that gives an overview is ideal. Drive to these points and simply look at the country. If you're on foot, it's not quite so easy, of course, but anytime I hike into new country to hunt, I first climb to the top of the highest ridges just to look around. It's time and energy well spent.

From any good vantage, use your binoculars to inspect the vegetation and terrain. You'll spot benches, basins, pockets of heavy timber, meadows, alder draws, north slopes and other features that might attract elk. And don't forget to look for elk themselves. If you watch at daybreak and dusk, chances are good you'll spot herds feeding in the open, and right there you've saved yourself many miles of walking.

Also when scouting, drive every road in the area or hike and ride the trails. That might seem like a waste of gasoline or energy, but familiarity with the road and trail network will contribute immeasurably to your hunting efficiency.

One other thing as you're scouting: Take time to chat with anyone you meet. One tip from a local could make your trip. One year my friend Larry Jones was bowhunting when he met a man scouting for the rifle season. They struck up a conversation and the man mentioned where he'd seen a 7-point bull. Larry made a mental note, and the next day he drove to that location and found that very elk. He saved himself many hours of scouting by being friendly. Never pass up the opportunity to chat with other hunters, loggers or foresters.

When you first arrive in an area to hunt, it is vitally important to get an overview of the country. This will help ensure a more successful hunt.

Maps. Another valuable scouting tool is maps. With topographic maps, an item you should never be caught without, you can do much of your scouting while sitting in camp. Look for basins, benches, north slopes, saddles, heavy pockets of timber, springs, heads of creeks and other localities that would provide the feed, water and cover desired by elk.

In many cases you can pinpoint the location of animals before you even look at the country. As an example, in Wyoming's Wind River Range, Roger Iveson and I sat by a warming fire one afternoon, lost in the fog. Visibility was less than 50 yards. This was our first time there so neither of us knew the area, and since we couldn't see our surroundings in the fog, we were basically lost. This was a major problem.

"Let's look at the map," I suggested. "Maybe we can get some ideas from it." We found our location on the map right beside a river. Just across the river, on a north-facing slope, the

A good topographical map and know-ing how to use it will reveal the most likely hunting spots. A map can be read at camp or while you're out on your quest like this hunter.

map showed three small drainages. At the lower ends they were very steep, but higher they flattened into small bowls. They looked good for elk.

"Let's cross the river and hike into those basins," I suggested. "Unless you've got a better idea."

"We could sit by the fire," Roger laughed. "But then, we probably won't kill any elk here, so let's go."

In the dense fog we needed a compass to find our way up the steep ridge, but as the terrain flattened out we knew we had hit the first basin. We bugled there several times and got no response, so we hiked on to the second. We bugled and a bull responded instantly. To make a long story short, we called in the bull and Roger nailed him. In many cases, you can use maps in that way to discover likely elk haunts.

As you scout, note wind patterns, too. Wind may be the most significant influence on your hunting plans, because you can't fool an elk's nose. Within a given area the wind generally has definite patterns, so try to map these out as you learn the territory, and use this knowledge later as you plan day-to-day strategies.

After a couple days of such scouting, you'll have an overview of the land and know specific localities that might hold elk. You can now set up camp in a central location and plan your hunt.

Reading Sign

One final step in scouting is reading sign. In most cases you'll simply combine this step with hunting, evaluating sign as you travel from one likely spot to the next.

Tracks and droppings are the most obvious sign. In general, elk tracks look like overgrown, blocky deer tracks. First try to determine the freshness. If the tracks are frost crumbled, you know they're at least a night old. If they've been rained in, they were made before the latest storm. If there's snow on the ground, you should be able to tell whether the tracks have been frosted or snowed in, or whether the wind has blown snow into the tracks. Press your fingers into the mud, snow or dust to give yourself a "freshness" comparison.

A yearling cow's tracks are about 3 inches long, those of a cow or small bull are 3½ inches long, and the tracks of a large bull are 4 inches or longer. Rounded tracks don't necessarily mean "bull." The front hooves on all elk are broader and more rounded than the hind hooves. I've measured several and have found that on large bulls, the front hooves are 4 inches long and 4 inches wide, and they're blocky almost like the hooves of a domestic cow. The hind hooves are also 4 inches long, but they're only 3½ inches wide and have the pointed appearance of deer hooves. The same general shape relationship holds for all elk. I measured the hooves on a yearling, for example, and the front hooves were 3 inches long and 3 inches wide; the back hooves were also 3 inches long, but they were only 2¾ inches wide.

During spring and summer, elk eat green grass and their droppings look like small cow pies. When the animals are feeding on browse, which generally is the case in the fall, their droppings are in the form of pellets. Usually they're about the size of olives, and a bull's pellets are dished on one end, like a pitted olive.

Fresh droppings are green and soft. In damp weather they might stay green for some time, but the inside will harden up. In dry weather, droppings will turn black quickly. If they're still moist inside, however, you know they've been made within the last day or two. If you find fresh tracks and droppings, rest assured that elk are nearby. Unless disturbed and run out of the country, an elk herd will stay in a small vicinity for a long period of time.

During the rut, you'll look for other sign, too. Rub trees are very common where bulls battled trees and shrubs. Don't ignore rubs; but don't put all your faith in them either, because the bull could have moved on. A rub doesn't mean much unless it's accompanied by fresh tracks and droppings.

Wallows where bulls have rolled in the mud also should catch your eye. If the water in a wallow is still muddy, you know a bull has used it recently and he may still be nearby.

On Your Own

With mere words on paper, no one can teach you how and where to hunt elk. However, the ideas outlined here have served me well in planning more than a dozen, self-guided elk hunts. Even with careful planning, your first hunt or two might prove frustrating, but on the other hand, you might start out like my friend Mike Gerber from Nevada.

Mike had hunted deer extensively, but he had no experience with elk. He bought a book on elk hunting and listened to several tapes, and he made a number of telephone calls to Colorado to get information on different areas.

He drove to northwest Colorado the day before the bow season opened and set up camp. Early opening morning he pulled on his camouflage clothes, painted his face and hurried up the mountain toward a promising aspen park. He blew his bugle and got an immediate response. At first he felt sure it must be another hunter, but he wasn't positive, so he set up and bugled again. In a short while, a bull arrived on the scene and Mike brought him down with an arrow. He had hunted a good full hour!

I can't promise you that kind of success, but if you'll follow the guidelines above and persevere long enough to learn, I think you'll enjoy some fantastic elk hunting—on your own!

9

Rangefinding Facts And Fallacies
by Bob Hagel

Range estimation and projectile drop have given hunters fits ever since our cave-dwelling ancestors first discovered they could send a flint-tipped stick to longer distances by using another stick bowed by a thong tied to each end. Soon they found that while the stick with the sharp rock point would penetrate and kill animals at rather long distances, the hunter still had to figure out how high it had to be pointed above the intended dinner to find the mark. They surely didn't visualize the range in yards or meters; however, it could be that this is when the value of pacing off distance took root in our history.

With the invention of gunpowder, guns and the round ball, the range at which animals could be hit and killed started to increase. As the accuracy and killing power of the round ball increased, so did the desire to shoot it at longer distances. The accuracy to hit an animal, and the punch to kill it at longer ranges are of little value if the hunter can't figure out how much the ball will drop below point of aim at the extended range, or, in fact, what that range actually is in yards.

As the years passed, the round ball was replaced by the conical bullet, and the smoothbore muzzleloader gave way to the rifled tube. The metallic cartridge soon followed. Soft lead-cores were clad in copper jackets, and smokeless powder backed them up for greatly increased velocity to afford even flatter trajectory and

This horizontal wire retical system indicates that this pronghorn is 300 yards distant if the buck measures 18 inches from back to belly. Because of the difficulty in precisely bracketing an animal, and size variation, such devices should be used for estimation only.

longer-range killing power. This should have made sure hits at longer ranges much easier, and it did. But as rifles and cartridges became more lethal at longer distances, exact estimation of distance became even more critical. Anyone with a little practice can learn to judge range to within a few feet at 100 yards, and with a bit more practice out to maybe 200 yards. However, at distances beyond that point it gets complicated.

But, tough range-judging conditions are not of any great concern to an experienced hunter if the animal is no more than a couple of hundred yards away. Even if it is farther away, say 300 yards, he is still in good shape with today's flat-shooting cartridges on big-game animals if the rifle is sighted in properly. He also isn't hurting too badly with most of the hot varmint cartridges if the guns are also sighted in correctly. Of course, there still are a lot of hunters and far too many guides who can't tell the difference between 200 and 400 yards. Beyond 100 yards, without the aid of a rangefinder, they are in trouble most of the time.

For hunting use, rangefinders come in two categories: the kind that are built within the hunting scope and are part of, or linked to, the sighting reticle; and the various instruments made for range estimation that are carried separately as part of the hunter's equipment.

Rangefinders Within The Hunting Scope

Rangefinders found within hunting scopes depend entirely upon game size for range estimation, while most of the instruments made especially for rangefinding use the split-image rangefinding approach—the same system used in many cameras based on the triangulation principle. As far as the hunter is concerned, the principle on which any rangefinding device is made is of little importance—it is how well it performs that counts.

First, let's take a look at the reticle rangefinders found within hunting scopes. The first rangefinder of this design is the Weaver double crosshair arrangement. There are two horizontal wires spaced to give a six-minute angle gap between them. This spacing is fixed and remains constant at all times, and at all ranges: 6 inches at 100 yards, 12 inches at 200 yards. When using this instrument, you must know the approximate depth of the animal's body from back to belly. Hold either the top or bottom wire on the back or bottom of the chest, and see how much of the body is left over, or how much it lacks filling the space between the wires. Then assuming you know the animal's body depth, you can estimate the distance by doing quick calculations in 6-inch increments. As an example, a buck deer is supposed to be 18 inches from hairline to hairline. If he fits snugly between the two wires, he is 300 yards from the rifle muzzle.

This all sounds quite simple and suggests quite accurate range estimation, but a number of bugs can contaminate the broth. As range increases it becomes more difficult to know how much daylight there is between the buck's back or belly and the corresponding crosshair. By the same token, it also becomes more difficult to hold the reticle steady, keeping it in perfect alignment with the back or chest line while estimating the amount of daylight seen in comparison with the animal's broadside view. Last, but not least, deer, like hunters, come in various sizes. There is a lot of difference in the body depths of various deer species and sub-species. Take mule deer as an example: Many young bucks are shot that will not measure more than 16 to 17 inches, while some

According to most information on deer body depths, an average buck is supposed to measure 18 inches from back to brisket. While this deer could well be considered average, he is certainly not in the trophy buck class, and much smaller than a big mule deer buck. Small bucks may not span more than 16 inches, while a big one may measure more than 22.

old bucks that are really in the trophy class will go in excess of 22 inches. Remember, we are not concerned with the vital area or the actual body depth, but with what we see from hairline to hairline. There will also be a difference of 2 to 3 inches in the same big buck from September, when he has just put on his fall, gray coat, to late November when that coat grows to winter length.

The picture becomes even more confusing when the average hunter, or even the long-time professional, tries a rangefinding reticle on other game: goat, elk, caribou, moose and bear. Not much published information is available to tell you how deep these animals are through the rib cage. The information that does exist normally shows even greater error than that available for deer. One source, for example, gives the depth of elk at 24 inches. If the fellow who made that measurement read his tape correctly, some areas must have elk that are a lot smaller than any I have ever killed. I've measured a number of mature cows that spanned more

One difficulty with reticle-type rangefinders is that they are dependent upon the "average size" of various animals. According to some sources, an average elk will run 24 inches from top of shoulder to bottom of chest, hairline to hairline. This one will run 32 or 33 inches, and some will measure a full 3 feet.

than that, and a lot of old trophy-class bulls that went 34 to 36 inches. If you misjudge an elk's body depth by a foot, the best rangefinding reticle ever made is of no use whatsoever.

Sure, there have been rangefinding reticle advances since Bill Weaver first produced his simple model, but they are still no better than the hunter's body depth estimation of the animal he is hunting. Take the stadia wire system as used in Redfield, Realist and some other scopes. I've tested most of them on objects of known size at various unknown ranges and then measured it off. They are very accurate if you have plenty of time and a steady rest, but you still have to depend on your knowledge of the animal's size to make use of that accuracy.

The advantage of the stadia wire system is, of course, that if you do have the time and can perfectly bracket the animal, it will tell you almost exactly what the range is. (That is, if you peg the hairline-to-hairline depth correctly.) Systems like the Redfield

Accu-Range give the range reading on the reticle setup, while the Realist Leatherwood hookup uses a cam arrangement that raises the elevation the right amount for the range. (That is, if the cam fits your particular load, including bullet ballistic coefficient and muzzle velocity.) But for a number of reasons, even these more sophisticated arrangements become increasingly more difficult to use when ranges extend beyond 300 yards or so.

With the stadia wire system, you don't have to guess the difference between what the two wires cover and the animal's depth ranges over, or under, the range where the fixed system brackets the animal. You can adjust the wires to bracket an animal of any depth at any range, and they either read that range or have it set automatically, whichever the scope provides. However, there is a little more to it than that. Even assuming you do know the animal's depth, you will still have to adjust the stadia wires to perfectly bracket it.

The first problem that occurs is the animal needs to be stationary and broadside (or nearly so). If the animal is facing toward or away from the hunter, it is extremely difficult to know when you are bracketing the body depth perfectly. If the animal is lying down, it is impossible to get a correct reading. It is also difficult if the animal is standing facing steeply either up or downhill. The second problem, and perhaps the most frustrating one, is finding a position where the rifle can be held steady enough for a perfect bracket while adjusting the stadia wires. A fellow testing one of the stadia wire scopes said that after a little practice he had no problem adjusting the scope from the offhand position. He either had more than his share of arms and hands, or would make a great Metallic Silhouette shot!

I don't seem to be able to do it accurately even when I'm sighting in on a cardboard box with straight lines, unless I have a steady rest and plenty of time. And, speaking of time, this is often a commodity there is precious little of. While you are doing all this fidgeting and adjusting, the buck, bull or ram may just start moving around or disappear. If it is already moving, either just meandering along or taking off, forget trying to estimate range with any kind of rangefinder.

One more point that has never endeared any of the stadia wire scopes to me is that they are all made in variable models, which usually means more bulk and weight. Although some hunters don't mind the ''extra'' load, I'm among those who do, and these scopes can be quite cumbersome.

Rangefinding Instruments That Hunters Carry

Now let's take a look at rangefinders that are made for the hunter to carry along while hunting. There have been a number of these over the past few years, most of which I have tested, and few of them still being marketed—which should tell the hunter something.

As mentioned earlier, most of these rangefinders are designed along with split-image range focusing systems similar to cameras without through-the-lens focusing. Accuracy depends upon the distance between the two viewing windows at the instrument's ends. The greater the range, the wider this spacing must be to retain accuracy, as well as the ease and speed in setting it. There is little reason to go into the several makes and models that have cropped up from time to time, because they are similar in principle and nearly all have the same failings as a useful tool to either the varmint or big-game hunter.

The best one I have tested to date is the recent Ranging Rangematic 1000, which uses a 6X monocular. One reason it is superior is because it is quite long with the windows nearly a foot apart. Of course, being long, it is pretty bulky and not especially light for a sheep or goat hunter to pack up a mountain. And the main problems I found in testing it were some of the same problems found in scope reticle rangefinders. True, you do not need to know the animal's size, because you twist a dial until his various parts fit tightly together, which is one up for the Rangematic. But you'll find that you do have to hold the instrument quite steady to accurately bring the two images together. As range increases, steadiness becomes ever more critical. After checking objects of all sizes and shapes, including many animals at various ranges, I found accuracy was good out to about 300 yards. After that, it became more difficult to obtain an accurate reading. It also became increasingly slow because you had to allow the needle to go back and forth past the reading a number of times to make sure you were correct. Even then, the range indication proved to be off more times than on (when checked against measured distances). After the range reached 500 yards, my best efforts were normally off by 50 to 100 yards, far too much to be of value on an antelope or deer.

Perhaps the biggest problem with this type of rangefinder is light. If looking across flat land with bright sunlight, the heat waves make it impossible to focus accurately. Also, if the animal is in shadow or blends in with the background, it is difficult to know

For top accuracy, any rangefinder will require the use of a steady rest when used at the longer ranges. Here, a fallen tree stump is used to steady the ranging "Rangematic 1000."

when the image is in perfect focus. (Close isn't good enough at long range.) Mist, rain and snow will also give you fits. Under any of these conditions, or at the longer ranges, it is time-consuming to take an accurate reading. And, even the specs on the instrument admit errors at ranges over 500 yards. By the time you feel fairly certain that you have an accurate reading, the animal you intended to shoot may no longer be in sight. Actually, this type of rangefinder is much more useful to the varmint hunter than to the big-game hunter for several reasons. For most varmint hunting, the extra weight and bulk matter little. Time is of little importance on ground squirrels, woodchucks and sod poodles. But because of the lack of time, these rangefinders are useless on jackrabbits and coyotes. Another reason they are more valuable to the varmint hunter is because they are accurate up to about 300 yards, which will cover the big-end of most varmint hunting.

One point that should be remembered in varmint hunting is that you'll hit few ground squirrels at 300 yards with the best varmint rifle and cartridge. And with the hot numbers that are capable of killing cleanly beyond that range, you'll have to do very little guessing to hit a woodchuck at 300 yards with proper sight settings. This means that if you sight a hot .22-250 load to impact 1.5 inches high at 100 yards, you can hold center of a feeding woodchuck and kill him every time out to about 275 yards. You can also kill him with a hold on the top of his shoulder at 300 yards. You'll find it hard to perfectly focus a rangefinder or a rangefinding reticle on a woodchuck at 400 yards.

In big-game hunting the same situation holds true, only more so. With cartridges in the range of the .308 Win. or even the .30-06, rangefinding equipment accurate up to about 300 to 350 yards could be quite useful if the hunter has time to use it. But with the flattest shooting numbers, it is of little value within ranges that should be considered by even the most qualified riflemen. There are three reasons for this. First, with cartridges that develop velocities of over 3,000 fps with bullets of good ballistic coefficient, and sighted to impact 3 inches high at 100 yards, you can hold in the center of the ribs and get a vital hit on a buck deer or ram at 325 yards or so, depending upon the bullet's actual velocity and ballistic coefficient. You don't have to do any range guessing, take any time adjusting stadia wires or other rangefinding apparatus, or try to figure the animal's correct size; you just hold dead center and touch it off. Second, not too many hunters can regularly hit a deer's vital area every time at more than 300 yards anyway. And third, if your cartridge isn't flat enough for this kind of sighting and holding at that range, it is not packing too much wallop when it gets there. This may cause the cartridge not to expand its bullets well enough at over 300 yards, which, in turn, prevents the tearing effect for killing shock.

If you use the right cartridge for shooting at long ranges where a rangefinder might prove handy, you probably do not have much use for the rangefinder, depending upon the limitations of your load and your own ability. Also, considering that the practical accuracy of either the reticle rangefinding scope or special range-finding instruments falls off badly at longer distances, as well as the often vital time consumed in using them, it seems they are of little value to the hunter.

Perhaps the greatest value of rangefinders, whether part of a scope or a separate instrument, is their ability to help the hunter who can't tell 150 yards from 400 yards. But, even then, he is better off using a flat-shooting cartridge and sighting it for the longest range possible without the bullet's path being too high at the midpoint in the trajectory, about 3 inches high at 100 yards. Then just hold center and forget about judging range. If the animal is so far away that the bullet lands low, chances are that the hunter couldn't hit the vital area if he did know the range and where to hold on the target. The hunter's judgment is important, with or without range-estimation devices. If your first instinct tells you that the animal looks too far away to hit in its vitals, then do not attempt the shot. A lot of wounded animals could be saved.

10

Locating Trophy Mountain Goats

by Lloyd Bare

O ne black hoof casually stepped ahead, then another. Exactly what supported the hooves escaped my detection. The blocky, pure white animal seemed to stroll on the side of the sheer Alaskan cliff. A fall meant a several thousand-foot tumble down the cliff. A look of amazement must have shown on my face as I watched the animal traverse the cliff without a care.

With no goat permit in hand, I set up my camera. Then the beautiful animal spotted me. He reversed direction without missing a step and strolled away. Even with the powerful telephoto lens I could see no means of support for the animal.

Suddenly the cliff face took a right angle turn. The goat calmly stepped across the chasm and continued. When whatever crack or tiny ledge he walked on ran out, the goat raised his front feet up to another slim foothold and pulled himself up. He disappeared around a corner but in a few minutes the goat spotted my hunting partner and started back in my direction. When he reached a position directly across from me, he nibbled on some unseen bit of vegetation on the rock. Never did the animal run or act spooked.

According to biologists, North America's Rocky Mountain goat (*Oreamnos Americanus*) probably crossed the Bering Sea land bridge in the middle Pleistocene period. Goats are closely related to the chamois of Europe but not to any species in North America.

Because of its rugged, alpine habitat, few early explorers saw any mountain goats. Lewis and Clark did spot the white animals in what is now Idaho. Alexander Henry saw and described the animals in the Kootenay, British Columbia, region in 1811. However, the animals were the subject of so many myths and legends that early biologists actually doubted their existence. By the late 1800s goats had been studied thoroughly in Montana. Again because of their remote habitat, goats are the least known and least understood animal by the public of any North American wild game.

For good reason, our native Indians called the mountain goat the white buffalo. Like the buffalo (bison), goats show a hump on the back. Also like buffalo, the animals are rather stocky. Behind the stocky body appears a short tail, in front grows a slender neck and rather smallish head. From the front or rear, goats appear slab-sided, which helps their cliff hugging and ledge walking.

An adult male mountain goat weighs up to 300 pounds, larger than most rams. Except during the early part of the hunting season, goats wear a long, heavy white coat. A 5-inch beard hangs below their chin and beautiful thick chaps cover a male's front legs. Mountain goats join Dall's sheep and polar bear as North America's only animals to wear a pure white coat year-round.

Both males (billies) and females (nannies) grow black, thin, pointed horns which increase in length each year until they reach 8 to 12 inches. Like ram horns, these little daggers lay down an annual ring each year and the horns are never shed.

A goat's skull is extremely fragile. Therefore, unlike rams, goats don't clash head-on. In fact, goats don't spar in fun like rams do. Their dagger sharp horns would kill another goat rather than just cause a headache. Goats seldom, if ever, fight. They only exhibit and false charge with their lethal horns.

Mountain goats are perhaps adapted better to their habitat than other wild game species. Their large, oval hooves include prominent dew claws so they can travel better through snow than sheep can. Their hooves consist of cushion-like pads surrounded by hard shell. The pads form suction cups on smooth rock surfaces giving goats their amazing climbing and ledge-walking ability. These great climbers seldom jump. Rather goats lever or pull themselves slowly up and down sheer cliffs from one foothold to another. In fact, they climb rock much like a man climbs a ladder.

Tracks left by a mature mountain goat are about the size of those left by deer and sheep but they print squarer and wider. They drop deer-sized pellets that appear concave on one end.

Rocky Mountain goats live in the high peaks, usually above sheep country. Because of their remote habitat, goats are arguably the least known and least understood wild-game animal.

Depending upon the area, nannies bear their kids in late May or early June. Normally they drop only one kid but occasionally twins are born. Nannies go off alone to a rugged area in the cliffs or occasionally a cave to drop their young. The precocious youngsters can follow their mother shortly after birth. In fact, they can climb anywhere their legs can reach within a few days of birth. Kids normally stay with their mother throughout their first year and into the second. Few, if any, goats live past 11 years.

You'll normally find goats above sheep in the highest, roughest terrain. As I write this, I remember the time I found goat hair on a spruce branch beside a lake at the bottom of the mountain. However, that's an exception. Mountain goats prefer steep slopes or cliffs which offer an untapped food source. No other animal spends forage time in goat habitat. The cliffs also offer protection from predators. No other animal, except man, can get around in goat habitat.

Because north- and east-facing slopes receive the most snow, they hold the most water and succulent forage in summer and fall. However, goats don't need open water because they can find snow year-round in good habitat.

A goat's diet varies from grass and brush to moss and lichens. During the winter months, goats stay on the lowest south-facing cliffs and high ridges where wind removes the snow.

Goats don't adapt nearly as well as sheep. They survive only in true alpine environments. But this same trait means that civilization has little or no effect on goat range, habitat or numbers.

Due to the harsh habitat and single births, mountain goats have never been numerous anywhere. Nor have their numbers been decimated like most North American species. Once a given habitat reaches its carrying capacity, mountain goat numbers remain fairly stable. Most biologists believe that the number of goats now living in North America is the same as it has been in the past.

No two animals living in such close proximity to each other exhibit such different personalities as do mountain goats and sheep. Wild rams spar with one another. They frolic across their alpine basins. They dash off in the presence of predators, including man. Goats on the other hand seldom run. In fact, they exhibit a noticeable phlegmatic personality. However, they can get around in country that would kill a ram.

Since mountain goats seldom stray far from their rugged habitat, they realize they can walk away from danger. Because they appear so slow and deliberate, many sportsman believe they can't see well. Actually they see as well as sheep but react differently. A goat thinks things out rather than dashing here and there, even after a shot. Because of the rugged terrain, goats, in the presence of danger, must choose an escape route with care and get out of sight the closest way. No animal in nature is more deliberate than our beautiful mountain goat.

On one of my first mountain hunting trips to British Columbia, I missed a fine goat with three shots due to some terrible shooting on my part. My guide, Dale Gunn of Don Peck Outfitters, and I sat near the top of a ridge watching the goat in the broken cliffs below. In response to the shots, the goat merely looked all around and then slowly backed away while I tried to reload. He put his front feet up onto a tiny ledge, pulled himself up 6 feet and disappeared into the cliffs. Never did the billy exhibit any panic or fear.

Dale and I moved lower and waited. Some time later, the goat came back out but didn't see us hiding behind a large boulder. This

Mountain goats join Dall sheep and polar bears as North America's only animals to wear a pure white coat year-round. This goat's summer coat will lengthen and thicken before winter.

time the shot was good. Mountain goats feel so secure in their alpine tors that they never panic or move fast.

Although several states offer from a few to many mountain goat permits, only Alaska, British Columbia, Idaho, Montana and Washington hold exceptionally high numbers of these mountain denizens. Due to their remote habitat, fish and game departments can offer no exact figures on goat populations, but fairly reliable estimates put the figure at between 12,000 and 20,000 goats in Alaska, 7,000 in Washington, 4,500 in Montana and over 3,000 in Idaho. British Columbia is home to perhaps 10,000.

Of all trophy headgear, goat horns rate perhaps the most difficult to judge, especially from a distance. Little difference exists between an average, mature goat horn and a record book trophy. Any billy carrying 9- to 10-inch horns is a good trophy and only an inch longer puts the trophy in the record book.

Two physical characteristics help the hunter judge the animal in the field. If the horns appear to be three-quarters the length of the head, the horns rate as good. Anything over three-quarters and you have a record. Although not a true measurement, a goat's ears in a normal position appear 4 inches long. Therefore, if the horns go twice as high as the ears, they should measure 8 inches. Also look for heavy bases for an exceptional trophy.

Further complicating trophy judgment is the fact that you have a difficult time determining the sex of a mountain goat until after the shot. Both males and females wear horns of similar length. Therefore, you may shoot either sex in most areas. Most sportsmen prefer a billy for both trophy quality and to preserve the species.

Male goats carry heavier horns with larger bases than females, although nannies may grow longer horns. In fact, at one time a nannie held the world record. In those days Boone and Crockett considered only horn length.

Although goats don't gather in large herds, as might be expected with either ewes or rams, normally nannies and kids stay in small herds of five or six animals. Unless a billy happens to wander by a group of females and young, he will usually be found alone. Male goats don't herd together with other males as rams do. Keep in mind, however, that you may see an old, dry nanny alone. A nanny's horns bend back more sharply than a billy's which curve evenly back as they grow.

Measure a goat's horns much like you do a ram's. Measure the length of the horn from the lowest point in front, over the outer curve to a point in line with the tip. Measure the base circumference at a right angle to the axis of horn. Do not follow the irregular edge of the horn. Then divide the length of the longest horn by four and measure the circumference at the first, second and third quarters. The total of the horn lengths and circumferences less any differences must score 50 to make the Boone and Crockett book.

As is the case with trophy sheep, heaviness in a goat horn counts for more score than horn length. In most cases a horn with a 10½- to 11-inch length and 5½- to 6-inch base will score high enough to make the book. The current No. 1 goat wears 12-inch horns with 6½-inch bases. After caping your goat don't forget to remove the remaining hide which can be used as a small, but beautiful rug.

According to knowledgeable sportsmen, mountain goats are perhaps our most underrated trophy and, in some areas, the most underutilized. Goats don't appear to be as much a magnificent

NAHC Member Chris Van Eimeren took this beautiful mountain goat with his .338 Win. Mag. in British Columbia. Each horn measured 10⅛ inches. Hunters find that goats are more phlegmatic than sheep when danger is present.

trophy as rams. Their little dagger horns don't have the mass or length of the rams. Their deliberate behavior doesn't excite hunters the way rams do. But the ebony horns against a snowwhite coat make a striking trophy.

Actually, mountain goat hunting presents much more demanding physical effort, especially climbing, than sheep hunting. Following a goat also can offer a much more dangerous route than sheep. Unfortunately, the hunting popularity of most North American wild game is based on peer suggestion rather than actual trophy quality.

The late Grancel Fitz felt much different about the quality of goat hunting than most sportsmen. "The peaceful, placid mountain goat is my personal candidate for the most dangerous game in the world. To those who might nominate the markhor or the ibex, African and Asian mountain game, I'll give respectful attention. Others can hold their peace. Mountain sheep have led me into tricky places where I was frankly scared. But goats, more than once, have had me within a whisker of being killed so that there is nothing funny even about the memory. No wounded African buffalo can kill you any deader than a thousand-foot involuntary swan dive onto a rock slide,'' Fitz wrote.

In his marvelous old book, *North American Head Hunting*, Fitz claims that goat hunters, especially neophytes, need to have a specially-selected guardian angel, one that pays no attention whatever to union hours. During his first goat hunt, Fitz and his guide returned to camp by separate routes. He at last realized that daylight would be gone before he could reach his regular creek crossing.

"So in the gathering dusk I went straight down to the canyon and luckily found a place where it was possible to cross the rushing stream and climb the wall on the other side. My guide had offered to carry my rucksack, containing my coat, a flashlight and a spare sandwich. My route lay parallel to the canyon, and when I had covered half a mile I came to a formation of granite that thrust outward from the mountainside until it became a sheer bluff rising from the creek.

"A nice ledge, almost two feet wide, invited me to try to get across the face, and when that ledge pinched out I scrambled up to a narrower one. Before I had gone very far I had been on ledges at six different levels. And then my troubles began.

"Clouds scudded across the sky, and the starlight was blotted out. Remembering that the creek was a long way straight down, I didn't dare to go on. But I had changed ledges too many times, and in this new darkness I didn't dare go back either. So I sat down on my ledge, and as I rested a little, thinking things over, it began to snow. In just a few minutes, the storm had developed into a howling blizzard, and the face of that cliff became a very poor place to spend the night. Somehow, I had to get out of there.

"Feeling for holds that I couldn't see, it was easier and safer to go up, and to feel the way better I took off my gloves. The going was painfully slow. My fingers, soon numb from the cold job of exploring snow-filled crevices, had to be warmed in my mouth. I followed the mountaineer's rule in reaching for a new hold with but one hand or foot at a time so that I always had three points of support.

"After some three hours of terribly slow but constant climbing I found a rock chimney, and when I had gone up it for about 30 feet I found that the top was blocked. Its walls were icy. I didn't

For many people, the peaceful, placid mountain goat is the most dangerous game in the world. "No wounded African buffalo," wrote Grancel Fitz, "can kill you any deader than a thousand-foot involuntary swan dive onto a rock slide." The sheer cliffs behind this goat are typical of prime goat habitat.

like the thought of going down, and in trying to get out at the top I very nearly fell. There is nothing spectacular about that, is there? Not the same thing as a wounded, charging tiger dropping dead a yard from a hunter with a jammed gun. But had I slipped just a shade farther, there would not have been many bounces in a dizzy plunge to the creek bed and a tiger couldn't have spoiled my evening more thoroughly.''

Fitz finally descended that chimney without accident and after another hour managed to climb over the top. Then after stumbling through a dense jack pine timber, wandering back and forth through a meadow in the dark and the swirling snow and falling in a creek several times, Fitz made it back to camp.

A few days later Fitz and his guide spotted a goat and decided to try for it. The guide suggested he go on ahead and find the best stalk. He told Fitz to climb as fast as he could and when he reached a certain point to come straight toward the bluff to meet him.

"A moment later I started after him, climbing on a slight angle toward the cliffs, and before long I came to a chute, a dry, narrow watercourse grooved into the mountainside by the melting of winter snows. Although it was only about 8 feet wide, it was much too steep and smooth so I went on up beside it until I saw three protruding stones about the size of my head studded across the chute with the middle one as a sort of apex above the other two,'' Fitz wrote.

"With my stick I prodded each in turn, testing them, and they seemed solid. The faces of these stones were flat, but the soil had been scoured away from the top edges, leaving an inch or two exposed. With my inside foot I stepped out onto the nearest, worked my hand across the slope until I hooked my fingers over the top of the higher one in the middle, then swung my outside foot across to the far stone, a scant couple of feet from the opposite timber. Not far to go, but spraddled out as I was, facing the chute, I needed one more purchase to balance myself. With the stick in my free hand I drove hard at the gritty earth to plant it firmly.

"On the sunny slope of the opposite mountain I had been doing that all afternoon. On this shadowed northern face, the ground was frozen solid. The point of my stick glanced off.

"I tried again, jabbing harder, and that dead stick broke off an inch below my hand and zoomed 700 feet down the chute to the rim of the canyon, where it leaped out into space for the sheer drop into the rocky creek bed.

"Feeling a little wobbly I attempted to back off, but there

A guide's pack horse will aid in getting your mountain goat back to camp. No hunter, especially a first-timer in goat country, should go anywhere without his guide.

wasn't room on the back stone for both feet. Just as I was trying for a solid foothold, my slung rifle had to swing awkwardly and I nearly went sailing down after my stick. It couldn't have been closer, and when, a split second later, I found myself in my original spraddled position, I almost fell off anyhow through sheer trembling. After an instant I steadied. I had to. But I thought no more about backing off.

"There was one other possible way out. If I could get both feet onto the far stone, which had a wider top, I might work my free hand ahead on the earth of the chute so that it would balance me while I let go the middle stone and made the short step to safety. When I felt cool enough I tried it.

"All went well until I had both feet planted on the farther foothold. Then, under my full weight, the stone under foot made a little crunching sound and began to come loose. How I managed it I don't know yet, but in a flash I was hung up on my three stones just as before. This time, though, I was putting very little weight on the loosened one.

"I was scared stiff—probably more scared than I've ever been before or since—but curiously, there was no trembling. Somehow, subconsciously, that lesson had been learned. I knew that without help I wasn't going to try to get off again, either forward or backward. There was nothing to do but stay there, and even that couldn't be managed indefinitely.

"Ten minutes, ten years, ten centuries later I heard the guide coming back. In another minute I grasped the stout stick that he extended, and my predicament was only a deeply etched memory," Fitz wrote.

I quote these rather lengthy passages from Fitz's book only to point out the danger and excitement inherent in goat hunting. And also to reinforce the suggestion that no hunter, and especially a first timer in goat country, should go anywhere without his guide. In the first chapter I related my terrifying experience on my first goat hunt when I tried to go down the mountain on my own. Don't attempt such folly. Your guide knows the mountain. He knows possible pitfalls and blockages. You don't. Any big-game hunter may find himself in a tight spot but I know of no other hunting that offers so many life-taking chances as goat hunting.

Tom Brakefield in his excellent book, *Hunting Big-Game Trophies*, reports his own terrifying experience with goats. He'd made a good lung shot on an old billy but the goat picked his way across the slope and disappeared into a chimney, completely hidden from view. After a lot of hard work, Brakefield and his guide made it to the chimney, but the goat wasn't in sight.

"We started up the edge of the chimney, staying as much as possible out of the treacherous loose rock and scree that could whisk us right off the steep incline. I led the way so I could shoot without hesitation. Suddenly, almost at the top of the chimney and about 100 feet directly above us, the goat hoisted himself to his feet and lumbered toward the top. There was no time, in three steps he would be over. So it was now or never—more like jump-shooting a cottontail than making the classically deliberate long-range mountain shot.

"I shot, the goat faltered, stumbled and then—almost in slow motion—sailed out into space and hit the loose scree 10 feet below where he had been standing, madly sliding and tumbling our way. We flattened ourselves against the wall of the chimney, fortunately finding a little shelter in a crack there as the goat flew by close

Spike camps high in the mountains make goat hunting much easier. Keep your camp out of sight in the trees if possible.

enough to touch. His mad, 200-foot slide stopped only against the final rock between him and a 500-foot vertical drop. We shook and puffed, both scared to death and glad to still be alive. My knees wouldn't work right and I had to pause for several minutes to recover enough in order to pick my way safely down to the goat. But today, each time I look at that head on the wall, I recall the goat that brought us within 18 inches of eternity.''

No, mountain goats may not possess the majestic headgear of the ram, nor the craftiness of the whitetail, nor the wariness of the elk. But they offer a beautiful, exciting and sometimes dangerous hunt in the rugged crags at the top of the world.

11

Pheasant Hunting Throughout The Season

by Bill Miller

Streets in Dodge City, Kansas, never really quiet down on the eve of the pheasant season opener. There is always some group of enthusiastic bird hunters about, preparing in their own way for the equivalent of a religious holiday.

Every hotel room has been booked for months. Restaurants stock up on extra provisions. Taverns and nightclubs double or triple the beer deliveries.

Hunters hit town in every conceivable conveyance. They drive into town in Suburbans and Broncos towing six- and eight-dog trailers. They fly in private planes into Dodge City's small airport. They take commercial flights into Wichita and rent cars to drive across the state in the gathering dusk.

The Kansas pheasant season opens on the morn, and quite conceivably hunters from all 50 states have gathered to salute this American rite of autumn. Such is the powerful allure of a brash and brassy bird called the Chinese ringneck pheasant.

In the next 48 hours about one-third of the total pheasant harvest for the season will be gathered. That's despite the fact that the season will run for more than two months!

And it's not just a phenomenon unique to the Sunflower State. The scenes are the same whether the town's name is Creston, Iowa; Pierre, South Dakota; or Lincoln, Nebraska. The pheasant season is a huge economic boon to these and countless big and small communities in the Midwest and Plains States. Everyone, from the hotel owner who hosts the same hunting guests yearly to the housewife who sets up a bird plucking service in her garage, counts on the pheasants and the pheasant hunters. For them, there is much more at stake than ''sport.'' For them the quality of life depends to some degree upon the pheasants.

But there is another kind of pheasant opener, too. One in which a boy and his dad load a springer into a pickup, drive a mile or two and hunt. No fancy preparation. No huge outlay of dollars. No long drive or airline flight through the night. But they appreciate the hunt just as much, and opening day is just as much of a holiday—it's just celebrated in a different tradition.

No other upland bird offers such diverse hunting opportunities in as many parts of North America, whether you're hunting in a large group or hunting on your own. Whether you're hunting in the wild, on put-and-take public lands or on licensed shooting preserves. Whether you're hunting driven birds or flushed birds. Whether you're hunting with a pointer, with a flushing dog or dogless. Or whether you're hunting grasslands, cornfields, hardwoods or pine belts. The pheasant provides just about any kind of hunting for which you could ask.

Upland purists will laud the civilized attributes of hunting ''Gentleman Bob'' and the trickiness of the wingshooting afforded by the ruffed grouse, but for the take-it-as-it-comes upland bird hunter, the loud garb and raucous cackle of the rooster pheasant is what autumn and upland hunting are all about.

The Ringneck Pheasant In North America

Even though the traditions of ringneck pheasant hunting in America's heartland are as truly red, white and blue as Mom and apple pie, the bird itself is not. The ringneck pheasant is not native to North America. He's a foreigner. Wildlife biologists call him an exotic.

For most folks today, it's difficult to remember a time when pheasants weren't part of the countryside in states like North and South Dakota, Kansas, Iowa, Nebraska, Minnesota, Wisconsin and Illinois. But it wasn't until the early 1880s that the first successful stocking of pheasants was made in the United States. Those birds were released in the Willamette Valley of Oregon by a gentleman named Judge Denny.

It's a sobering thought for the pheasant devotee to imagine this marvelous game bird never coming to American shores. And it's

The ringneck pheasant, a foreigner to North America, is today an important financial boon to many Midwestern communities.

not that far-fetched to think that if the exotic laws back in the late 1800s were as strict as they are today, we wouldn't have a wild pheasant population in this country.

The ringneck pheasant's original homelands are the grassy steppe regions of Asia, particularly Mongolia.

Upland bird populations are incredibly dynamic, fluctuating in huge swings depending upon habitat loss or gain, weather and predation. In considering the history of the ringneck pheasant in North America, most veteran hunters and farmers agree that the real heyday of the pheasant in North America was the 1940s through the early '50s.

Take Wisconsin for example. The first planting of pheasants in Wisconsin took place in 1916 when Colonel Gustav Pabst made releases in the fields of Waukesha and Jefferson counties in southeastern Wisconsin. The birds took, and 11 years later Wisconsin held its first open season on pheasants in those two counties.

Encouraged by the success of Pabst's stockings, the old Wisconsin Conservation Department (the predecessor of the Wisconsin Department of Natural Resources) decided to get in on the act. It opened a state game farm at Peninsula State Park, expressly for rearing pheasants. In 1934, the operation was moved to larger facilities in Poynette.

During the '20s and '30s Wisconsin's primary reason for stocking pheasants was expansion of their range, and by 1942 the birds were present in all but 11 of the state's northernmost counties where habitat is not suitable.

Even though 1942 was a war year, Wisconsin hunters harvested an estimated 801,000 birds. Never before or since have Wisconsin pheasant hunters done as well!

At present, Wisconsin is a marginal pheasant hunting state at best. More recent goals in Wisconsin have been to maintain a statewide population of about 385,000 roosters. That's a total population figure, not a harvest figure!

Other states like the Dakotas, Iowa and Kansas have fared much better and offer more pheasants to the modern upland bird hunter. But even in these premier pheasant states you'll seldom hunt a whole weekend of the season without running into a lifelong farmer who will regale you with tales of flushing hundreds of pheasants from a single weedy draw! To some extent these may be embellished tales of a lost youth—hunting stories. But to inspire such a plethora of common stories, these scenes must have been witnessed at least a few times in "the good ol' days."

Wherever pheasants have fallen on hard times, temporarily or over the long haul, the primary culprit is loss of habitat. Fencerow to fencerow farming, the early mowing of hayfields and the pesticides which sweep corn rows completely weed-free, all steal valuable nesting and wintering habitat from pheasants. As farmers have sought to squeeze every bushel of production from the land in tough economic times, these pheasant-killing practices become more and more common.

Thankfully, game departments and folks who love pheasant hunting aren't languishing in remembrances of the past halcyon of the pheasant. They are out trying to make good new days.

Game departments have wisely seen fit to require hunters to purchase "pheasant stamps" with the revenue from their sale earmarked specifically for pheasant habitat recovery. Organizations like Pheasants Forever are in the forefront of the private sector to support pheasants and pheasant hunting. It's their efforts, with our support, that we must bank on. It's through them that we'll keep the all-American tradition of pheasant hunting alive. All pheasant hunters should try to get involved in some way or another. Check locally for organizations.

Opening Day Pheasants

There are all kinds of opening day pheasants. Despite what others may say, you can't pin them down and say, "All opening day pheasants always do this," or "All opening day pheasants always do that." The birds are as individual as hunters and react to opening day hunting tactics in an infinite variety of ways. On opening day, and throughout the hunting season for that matter, pheasants will react based on any number of criteria. Some include the amount and type of cover, weather conditions, hunting pressure and previous experiences, if any, with hunters.

All successful upland bird hunting keys on two components. One is locating the birds; two is getting them to behave the way you want them to.

This holds true from the first time you uncase your shotgun on opening day, until you encase it after the final hour of the season.

For the upland bird hunter, especially the guy who will be hunting on opening day, locating the birds is usually not a problem. The out-of-state hunter most likely will be hunting with a local contact whether that's a friendly farmer, a guide or a long distance friend. You can rely on them to help you find birds. If you'll be relying on your own reconnaissance, you will find then that a bit of preseason scouting is in order.

Scouting for pheasants is really no different than scouting for big game. You can use maps and game department reports to get you going, but the best way to find birds is to get out there and look for them. Drive back roads in the area you hope to hunt and look for pheasants.

Don't make the mistake of looking only in the road ditches. Take along a pair of binoculars to glass open grain fields and distant fencelines. It's best to do your scouting at the times birds feed or gravel. They are most active then and easiest to spot.

An increasingly important part of preseason scouting for pheasants is to secure landowner contacts. Who owns that piece of land where you saw eight roosters perched in the hedge apple bushes along the roadside one foggy morning? Will he let you hunt it? These are questions to answer two or three weeks before the season opens—not in the last hour before opening!

Scouting well before the season opens gives you time to check out all your sources thoroughly. A friendly mailman who carries over a large rural route can be a tremendous resource of bird population information. In fact, many states rely on the counts made by postal carriers to determine game bird populations. Since he delivers mail, he may also be able to point out the landowners of specific parcels.

Sheriff's deputies who patrol rural roads, milk truck drivers who pick up at even the most remote farms, fuel oil delivery men—all are potential gold mines of information on pheasant populations and locations. Use your imagination and you can probably come up with several people you know who have the opportunity to travel country roads a lot.

And when someone provides you a hot tip, don't forget to thank them. A sausage, some cheese and a smoked pheasant or two go a long way toward showing your appreciation, and to securing their future hot tips.

Using all the resources available and some serious reconnaissance on your own makes scouting the easier of the two components for a successful hunt. Even in lean years when pheasant populations are down, you'll find birds to hunt if you get out there ahead of time and look for them.

Component No. 2—getting the birds to act the way you want them to—is far more difficult. That's the component that makes hunting exciting.

To the devout pheasant hunter, nothing compares to the traditions of opening day. Scenes like this are what keep hunters going through the rest of the year.

What kind of birds are you dealing with on opening day?

More than any other time during the season, you'll be working young, inexperienced pheasants. Not dumb pheasants—young and inexperienced pheasants. By the time hunting season rolls around, there really aren't any dumb pheasants. Mortality on first-year birds caused by predation and the vagaries of weather is so high that dumb birds do not survive very long.

If pheasants could pass their hunter-wariness from generation to generation, very few would be taken by nimrods who ply the fields! Actually, it's not too farfetched to believe that this could be happening genetically. If a pheasant has in his genes a tendency toward running instead of flying, he is likely to live longer and breed more than his flying kin. That means he'll be passing his traits on to more descendants than the flying bird. Theoretically, over the lifetimes of many hunters, we could be left with a race of running pheasants that seldom take to the air!

That aside, your best bet for encountering inexperienced pheasants is on opening weekend and during the first week of the season. It's at this time that what have become "traditional" pheasant hunting methods work the best.

Even so, careful attention to detail in your hunting strategy will produce faster action and more birds brought to bag.

The Opening Day Drive

For many upland bird hunters, the opening of pheasant season means getting together with a large group of friends to work together to bag some birds—and, more importantly, to have a good time. Like any other convening of a hunting fraternity, there is a great deal to be said for the camaraderie of this kind of hunting. Friends and relatives in a pheasant hunting gang may see each other only once a year, barring weddings and funerals, but they'll list those seldom seen cohorts among their very best friends.

And there's more to be said for opening weekend drives. Properly executed, they can produce outstanding hunts with lots of shooting for everyone.

The most important key to success in any driven hunt, whether for pheasants or deer or any other type of game, is a good leader. An effective hunt leader must be a hunter who is familiar with the birds and the land to be hunted, and who is persuasive enough to get everyone in a large, diverse group of excited, anxious hunters to strive for the same goal: a safe and enjoyable hunt for all. The best hunt leader is often the landowner who is hosting the hunt or

As land access becomes more difficult, it is extremely important to thoroughly scout areas during preseason. Your odds for a successful hunting trip will increase if you are prepared.

the individual who is the group's organizer.

Safety is of paramount importance on any hunt—especially a large group hunt. You can never be quite sure of what you're getting into in a large group. There are always newcomers from whom you don't know what to expect and there are some hunters who tend to become lax about safety precautions as they become comfortable with a group. Keep out a watchful eye for both.

The first and most important job for the drive hunt leader is to lay down some basic, inflexible safety rules for the hunters in the group. Rules should include, but are not limited to the following:

1. All hunters must wear a blaze orange hat and at least a blaze orange vest above the waist.

2. All shots taken by drivers or standers must be above the horizon. That means that sky must show below the barrel when swinging on a bird.

3. Drivers must stay aware of the positions of the hunters on both sides and should not walk ahead or fall behind the line.

4. Standers must stay in their positions until the drive is absolutely finished, meaning that the drivers have passed the line of standers.

5. When a walker drops a bird, the rest of the drive line should stop while the two or three hunters closest to the mark move in quickly to retrieve the bird.

6. Standers should carefully mark fallen birds, but use caution about retrieving them immediately as the drive line approaches the end of the field. It's best to have two or three hunters designated on each drive to assist standers in marking and retrieving fallen birds.

A short meeting after breakfast on opening morning is often the best forum in which to present these laws of the day. And it's not "too much" to have a chalkboard handy to draw out what you're talking about. Make sure that there is an opportunity to get the safety points across before guns are uncased and the hunters are shuffling their feet in impatience to hunt.

These rules may seem like common sense, but they must be reiterated several times before the group goes afield. Opening day pheasant drives can be big, really big, with 50 hunters or more joining forces to hunt large fields. Safety can't be emphasized enough.

Besides, some of the same rules that will make a hunt safe will also make it more successful.

For example, keeping drivers in a straight row shortens the distance between drivers, making it less inviting for crafty pheasants

Opening day pheasant drives attract large groups of hunters. For many hunters the group camaraderie is what pheasant hunting is all about.

to run back between the walkers and hide or flush behind the line. Having blockers refrain from searching for fallen birds until the drive is over will keep them alert for more birds that may happen to come by.

Attention to detail can make the difference to the success of an opening day pheasant drive. The same field, carefully pushed by a group of diligent, concentrating hunters, might produce twice as many birds as if it were pushed by hunters moving too fast in a ragged line who are not really thinking about what they are doing.

A successful pheasant drive is slow. The birds are more reluctant to run back through a slow moving line of hunters than a fast one.

The distance between drivers is best dictated by the type of cover. In standing corn, as in Iowa and Nebraska, a walker in every fourth or fifth row may not be enough. Hunting cut milo fields in western Kansas, hunters could be spaced as much as 20 to 25 yards apart. Especially when drivers are sparse, flushing dogs like labs and spaniels do well to fill in the gaps. When drive hunting, it is of the utmost importance to have a well-mannered dog which obeys commands immediately and which will walk contentedly at heel when called upon to do so. Bringing an unruly dog along on a drive hunt is a very fast way to lose an invitation to hunt with the group again.

Next to running back through gaps in the line of drivers, the favorite evasive technique of the pheasant is to run ahead and around the end of the line. There are two good ways to combat this particular tactic.

If plenty of hunters are available, position some "standers" along the sides of the field being driven as well as on the end of it. As the drive moves down the field, the standers along the sides of the field join the line when it reaches them. The distance between drivers along the line compresses as more standers become walkers. This results in a tighter and tighter line of drivers as it approaches the blocked end of the field where the birds are most likely to try to sneak back through the line.

If the size of the group doesn't allow enough bodies to block the sides of the field, then the end walkers on the line should swing ahead of the line about 25 or 30 yards, and the drivers second from the ends should be ahead about 15 or 20 yards from the line to the inside of them. This presents to pheasants running to the sides of the main line the illusion that they are surrounded and that they can't circle to the outside of the drive without being detected.

Let the size of the group dictate the size of the fields to be hunted. A group of 50 or 60 hunters can band together and effectively cover half-mile-square milo fields in two swings. That means each field would be driven approximately one half at a time. The driving line would be about a quarter mile wide and push a half mile of stubble field toward the posted blockers.

Smaller groups naturally must seek out smaller patches of cover to hunt efficiently. A narrow weedy ditch, swale, or fenceline could be driven effectively by as few as four hunters, or maybe less with a good dog.

Opening Day On Your Own

For some hunters the joy of the hunt is lost in a large group. To them, the tradition of opening day is hunting alone, with a single friend or a small, carefully chosen cadre of hunting soul mates. Often these are hunters with canine companions who get as much pleasure from watching the dogs work as in any aspect of the hunt.

Individuals and small groups of hunters can be very successful on opening day pheasants if they avoid the temptation of the huge fields of standing or recently harvested crops. It is even more important for the lone or small-group hunter to gear himself to the

The distance between hunters in a drive is dictated by the cover. In standing crop fields it's best to have a hunter every few rows to keep the birds from sneaking back through the line.

appropriate sized patches of cover. For anyone with doubts, imagine looking down from an airplane on a 5-acre patch of standing corn. Just think how little ground is covered at any one time by three hunters and two dogs in that patch. There is no reason that any pheasant in that patch would ever be forced to fly as an escape. (Some might do it anyway, but they're the ones that don't get to pass the genes to the next generation of roosters.)

Hunters who seek pheasants on their own or in small groups must take an analytical approach to large patches of cover. Within those large patches are smaller isolated segments of cover that can be effectively hunted. Some of the most obvious are weedy ditches and fencerows. Tiny sloughs are good, too. In states where it is legal to hunt them, road ditches are popular, too. Railroad rights-of-way offer some good opportunities if you can get permission to hunt them.

The small group hunter should think small and think narrow. It's surprising how many birds will flock into a small patch of cover if it provides the right elements to hold them.

The hunter on his own must also work to get birds to flush within range of his gun. The drive hunter doesn't have to contend with this problem as much because if the group is large enough and well organized, somebody is going to get shooting at every rooster which exits the field in the air.

To hold the birds closer, the individual or small group hunter does better to concentrate on thick cover. Pheasants tend to hold better in thick grass or weeds than in the sanitary rows of a chemically treated cornfield. Look for cover like cattails, plum thickets, and dense grass and weeds.

One of the neatest tricks a lone hunter or a small group of hunters can pull is to pick up birds that the drive hunters missed; birds that were right under their noses. For example, in western Kansas a great deal of milo (sorghum) is grown in fields watered by center-pivot irrigation systems. These systems usually consist of a one-quarter-mile-long irrigation pipe mounted on wheels. Water is pumped from the center out to sprinkler heads spaced along the length of the pipe. They call these fields "milo rings" because the system irrigates a half-mile diameter circle around the center of the field.

However, just like anywhere else, the roads in the Kansas countryside are laid out in squares around the fields. That means each milo ring has four corners which are often left fallow. Now that's perfect pheasant cover, but it's often pushed too fast or not at

Small groups or even individual hunters can enjoy opening day success if the hunt is well planned and executed. Knowing the terrain you will be hunting also is extremely important.

all by drive hunters who have developed tunnel vision for row crops. A hunter or two with a good dog or two can have a "field" day cleaning up these corners that weren't pushed properly.

For the best success, the individual hunter needs to know the intricacies of the terrain he is hunting. He can make great use of the land to get the birds to behave the way he wants them to.

A stretch of open ground and the end of some dense cover is as effective for the lone hunter as a row of blockers is for a drive hunter. Pheasants will tend to run ahead of hunters and dogs until they come to an open patch of ground. They know that if they cross the patch on foot they'll be as vulnerable as if they flew. Their first alternate plan would be to cut back past the approaching hunter if at all possible. With that alternative eliminated by a slow but steadily approaching hunter who is weaving his way back and forth through a narrow strip of cover, the next choice is to wait it out and hope the hunter doesn't come too close.

When a pheasant makes that decision he's as good as yours if your aim is true. (That is, if you walk out the whole cover!) Never stop short of the end of a strip of dense cover. Always pause for a few moments just inside the edge of the cover, and then for good measure walk out into the open. Very rare is the opening day cock pheasant with nerves steely enough to stay hidden when you've stopped and he's sandwiched between you and the wide open spaces. Chances are he's gonna fly, and you're gonna get him!

A New Approach For Mid-Season Pheasants

Ten days into the season, the rules change. Except on the most diligently guarded private property there are no inexperienced pheasants left. More of the crop fields may have been taken in, but if the weather hasn't cooperated, the farmers will have little more out of the fields than they did on opening day. Cold weather and snow probably have not arrived either, to concentrate the birds and force them into winter cover.

The conditions from this point until winter really sets in present some of the most difficult hunting the upland bird hunter is likely to encounter. He's dealing with hunter-wise birds that have huge tracts of cover in which to maneuver.

The way to score on pheasants during mid-season is to hunt with care and to become as unpredictable as the quarry. That means taking a new approach.

In analyzing a patch of mid-season pheasant cover, try to figure out how other hunters would normally approach the area, then do the opposite.

Consider the following scenario as an example.

You know of a farmer who has granted you permission to hunt his property in the past, so you stop to say hello and see if he'll oblige you again. After handshakes and friendly small talk, he tells you you're welcome to hunt, but most of his good areas have already been hunted that morning by his brother and nephews. However, you learn that he bought a new farm during the summer. It's about six miles away and hasn't been hunted since Sunday. It's Friday, so it sounds like it might be worth a try.

With another handshake you take the crude map he drew on a scrap of paper torn from a paper feed bag, and you're off to go hunting. The dogs whine in the crates; they're as anxious as you.

As you drive to this new hunting ground, you think of the other things your farmer friend told you. The place has been hunted about half a dozen times since opening day three weeks ago. The

Always walk a patch of cover to the very end. Birds will hold tight and never flush if you come up short. Shots are common at the end of cover.

landowner said the guys who hunted it didn't get many birds after opening day, but they have been doing a lot of shooting. In fact, he asked them not to come back because when he was over there picking corn, he found some fenceposts shot up pretty bad.

From what he showed you, your contact owns half the section. A paved road runs the mile along the south end that belongs to him. Just off that road, almost centered within that mile, are the abandoned buildings of the original farmstead. The grass that has grown where the driveway once existed is well matted down from farm machinery and the previous hunters who parked in the yard.

To the east of the buildings is a picked cornfield, which is bordered by a dirt road that runs north-south. To the west is a large plowed field. Directly behind the buildings is a small pond surrounded by head-high weeds. It sits at the foot of a long, weed-choked ditch which winds north from the pond toward the far side of the property. The ditch and the grassy lane next to it are about 20 yards wide in total. They separate the plowed field and picked corn, but grassy swales occasionally swing away from the ditch out into the cornfield.

About a quarter mile to the north of the pond the ditch widens into a large fallow area. It includes some timbered swales running north onto adjoining property which is heavily posted, but is mostly fallow crop land enrolled in the Conservation Reserve Program (CRP). (In other words, the farmer is receiving benefits from the government not to grow anything on that land.) It is 60 to 70 acres of prime mid-season pheasant cover. This unfarmed plot is sort of a U-shape separated from the road on the east by part of the cornfield and on the west by the plowed field and a dense fenceline of hedge apples.

Shifting into low, you pull your truck into the abandoned farm lot and reconnoiter. From the condition of the parking area in the farm yard, it's quite evident that every group of hunters to date have probably started and ended their hunts here. That means other than the gang which drove the cornfield opening day (then unpicked), everyone else who hunted this farm probably worked it the same way. They all hunted the ditch back to the CRP land, made some circles out there, then walked the edge of the cornfield back to the vehicles, occasionally pushing the grassy fingers back to the ditch. Depending upon the size of the groups, someone may have been blocking at the ditch, maybe not.

If that's true, the pheasants on this farm have been hunted at least five times in a row pretty much the same way. Imagine what those birds in that ditch will be doing the second they hear the tailgate of your pickup slam shut and the action of your shotgun close. They'll be running north and won't stop until they are on the safe side of the posted fenceline. Those that don't will flush way ahead at the first tinkling of the dog bells.

Though you're dealing with experienced birds, you have an advantage in that they only have experience with hunters doing things the same way over and over. You have the opportunity to add a new twist, and add some of those experienced pheasants to your bag.

You back the truck onto the highway and drive down to the dirt road along the edge of the cornfield. You turn left and follow the dirt road to the fenceline on the north side of the cornfield which marks the edge of your friend's property. You pull into the field on a service drive and park well out of the way of any machinery that might come in or out of the field.

Keeping the dogs on leashes, you and your two hunting pals ease the doors and tailgate shut and then walk quietly west on the south side of the fenceline. When you get to the eastern edge of the fallow land, one hunter stays near that edge and waits. You walk to about the center of the patch and stop. Hunter number three proceeds over to the western edge of the CRP ground.

At a predetermined time you all begin a slow, meandering hunt south. You give the dogs plenty of time to work out all the cover thoroughly. By the time you all meet at the top of the ditch, the total bag is four roosters with a couple more missed. The dogs got to work on a bunch of hens, too. Some cold soda is in order for the human hunters and the dogs get a well-deserved ration from the canteens.

Before break is over, the guy with the youngest legs finds the dead-furrow in the plowed field and hot foots it for the farmyard. He leaves his dog with you and the senior member of the group.

When you can see the kid's orange coat against the oak tree at the far side of the pond, you and the other hunter set out in that direction. Again, slowly. Your companion takes the ditch and lane with two dogs, while you and your pooch walk far out into the cornfield. At the top of the first grassy swale you meet, you work it back to the ditch where the ditch walker is waiting. As you move within 15 feet of him, two hens take wing.

"Gees, I almost stepped . . ." A rooster cackles and takes out behind you. You swing through and dump him. Your dog makes a great retrieve over the crest of the hill in the corn stubble.

You head back to the southeast through the corn and work the next swale back to your buddy in the ditch just the same way. You do this for each swale leading to the ditch. Finally, at the pond, you work around the east side and the older gent works to the west. The kid shows you both up when he dumps a double on the two long-spurred roosters that boil out because they've got no way left to turn.

The bag—seven big, beautiful, experienced rooster pheasants. The method—a new approach.

Almost any piece of cover can be hunted with a new approach. It may not be the most convenient way to cover a patch of ground. (In the example, you ended the most productive hunting more than a half mile from your truck.) However, the results will usually be worth the extra effort.

Careful attention to details can make or break any approach to a hunting area in mid-season. Avoid unnecessary noise or talking. Keep dogs at heel until you are absolutely ready to hunt and shoot. Take the time to hunt every piece of cover thoroughly. Take every opportunity to use a blocker and to use natural barriers that prevent birds from running ahead.

The lone hunter can try new approaches, too. For example, the lone hunter's chances of flushing an experienced pheasant from a long, heavy-cover ditch without the help of a blocker are slim. However, he can become his own blocker. After he has steadily pushed the ditch 100 yards or so he should watch ahead for a bend. A good distance before he gets to the corner, he should climb out of the swale on the inside of the bend. Doing double-time across the open field, he should loop ahead to the next bend, then climb back into the swale and work back in the direction from which he had been approaching.

Any pheasants that rounded the bend ahead of the hunter will still believe they are being pursued from behind, then suddenly run into what they think is a second hunter approaching from the front! They are fooled into feeling surrounded, and that's when pheasants opt for the last resort—flight. And again, with a new approach you've made experienced, mid-season pheasants behave the way you want them to.

The Tough Get Going

It takes a tough hunter to hunt tough birds. Hunters after late-season pheasants have to be among the toughest.

In most parts of pheasant country, late season is cold. And late

At any time during the season, the lone hunter will benefit from the assistance of a good dog. Keep your dog at heel until you are ready to hunt and shoot.

season pheasant hunting often means wading through snow, sometimes lots of it.

The birds are at their fewest and wariest. On top of that, they are concentrated. Most of the crops are out, and all of the birds are seeking thick protective cover adjacent to some kind of food source. The cover must offer shelter from wind and storms. The food must be close at hand so that the energy it provides isn't wasted in traveling great distances to and from feeding.

At this time of the season, though, the birds are the easiest to find, they are most difficult to hunt. The hunter after late season birds often has to deal with large numbers of sharp eyes and ears all on alert for danger. Because lesser cover is beaten down and/or covered with snow the birds can see farther. And when they are in the preferred, dense cover, an undetected approach is almost impossible.

Hunting late-season pheasants can be plain hard work. But the hunter willing to put in the time and effort can score consistently if he'll use the sound, basic techniques of early and mid-season hunt and combine them with some special late-season know-how:

1. In late season, seek out and hunt the thickest cover you can find. Two favorites are cattail sloughs and evergreen shelter belts. Even small patches of these thick cover types can hold unbelievable numbers of late-season roosters.

Hunting a December cattail slough for pheasants can be a strange experience. You may actually be hunting on the surface of a frozen marsh where you shot ducks over decoys just a few weeks before.

In shelter belts of dense spruce or pine, shooting late-season pheasants can be very much akin to hunting ruffed grouse. You take snapshots or you don't shoot.

2. Weather that's not fit for man nor beast is fit for hunting late-season pheasants. During late-season snowstorms, pheasants will stay in dense cover later into the day and they will hold tighter. Likewise, on extremely cold mornings they will tend to stay on their roosts longer.

Naturally, special precautions for hunters and dogs are necessary in this kind of weather. Check often for frostbite on humans and canines. Keep as little flesh as possible exposed to the wind. Check dog's paws often to keep snow from balling up between the pads. Keep chains and other emergency gear in the trunk. Be sure to have plenty of blankets and hot drinks close- at-hand, too. Dogs require more energy to stay warm, too, so make sure to keep them

Late-season pheasants favor heavy cover, and they'll often flush well out of range.
That means less shooting for the walkers and longer range shooting for the blockers.

as well fed as possible.

3. If you can gather enough hardy souls at this season, large drives can still be a successful technique in late season. A large cattail slough is a prime drive target in December or January.

Birds will flush much farther ahead of the drivers than they did on opening weekend. That means less shooting for the walkers and longer range shooting for the blockers. Tighter chokes, larger shot and magnum loads are the order of the late-season drive.

For safety, all drivers must still wear blaze orange; however, if the group is trustworthy enough and the blockers can be positioned in the open, consider asking the standers to deck themselves out in marsh grass camouflage or a snow pattern. The pheasants that will be flying their way may have survived earlier drives and they know what that stationary orange blob is all about.

4. Ambush comes into play in late season if a hunter can determine a route that is regularly used by pheasants moving from

protective roosting cover to feed areas. Depending upon the weather and their inclinations, pheasants may walk or fly between these areas. So while hunting out the route's ground cover, try to keep one eye on the sky for birds taking an aerial path.

Tail Feathers

Wherever and whenever the pheasant is hunted, it is a bird worthy of tremendous respect. It offers such a diverse range of hunting opportunities for so many hunters that the loss of this game bird would be a tragedy. The effects of that loss would not only be felt by the hunting community, but by the citizens of countless rural communities that rely on an annual influx of revenue from pheasant hunters.

Though the pheasant is making tremendous comebacks in many parts of its range, two factors contribute most to the loss of pheasant hunting opportunities. One is the decimation of nesting and wintering habitat; the other is the closing of private land to hunters. In a single season, either or both can wipe out pheasant hunting in a large area.

Thankfully, the hunter has some control over the first and almost complete control over the second. For the sake of those who cherish the grand old tradition of pheasant hunting and those who have yet to try it, pheasant hunters need to strongly support habitat restoration projects. And they must take it upon themselves to present shining examples of ethical and respectful behavior in the field and out of it.

12

Winning Turkey Set-Up Techniques
by John Phillips

The most important consideration when deciding where to set up
to call in a gobbler is to know where a turkey doesn't want to
walk. A gobbler prefers not to ...

... get his feet wet by crossing water.

... fly across water.

... walk through heavy cover or downhill.

... walk under a fence or fly over it.

... move into an area where he's encountered danger before.

... go into a region where he thinks another gobbler will beat
him in a fight.

If a sportsman sets up in any of these areas and tries to call up
a gobbler, chances are good that the bird won't come to him.

However, there are places a turkey enjoys walking. He is very
apt to walk in a clean woods with little underbrush and in fields
where he can see for great distances. He'll also walk on flat ground
whenever possible.

And a turkey follows a regular routine. He's like the old man
down the street who goes by the barber shop at 8:15 a.m., stops at
the hardware store to find out if anyone's sick, dead or just married,
swings by the coffee shop to pick up a newspaper and a sweet roll,
and then moves on to the fire station for a game of dominoes. You
can set your watch by that old man.

You can also set your watch by an old gobbler in the spring.

That bird has a set routine as predictable as the man down the street. Figure out that pattern and you'll probably bag the bird. He will roost in the same tree, fly down in the same direction, try to mate in his strutting zones and feed in the same fields.

Once you know the routine, it's time to plan the setup.

The Typical Setup

One of the problems that a novice hunter has when setting up on gobblers is that he tries to get too close to the turkey. The result is that the bird spots the hunter and moves out of the area well before the hunter even tries to call him in.

Most often this happens when a turkey gobbles in the direction of a hunter, turns around on the limb, faces the opposite direction, then gobbles away from the hunter. The bird then sounds farther away than he actually is. A good rule of thumb is to always set up farther away from the bird than you think you should.

Although a turkey is sometimes taken on the first setup, it's by no means typical. More often than not, the hunter must set up two or three times to call the turkey.

Successfully changing calling locations is tricky, but the most important concern is knowing when to move and when to sit still. Many hunters spook a turkey when, after a few minutes of calling, the bird doesn't come in so the hunter gets up and moves to another location. Often, the hesitant gobbler is spooked by the impatient hunter.

There are times, however, when the hunter must move or else he won't get a gobbler. Maybe there's a creek or ditch that he doesn't know about. Perhaps the gobbler has encountered some hens and started to walk out of the area. The turkey may be call-shy because of other hunter encounters. Or the old bird may just be ornery and decide, "If that hen wants to breed, she'll have to come find me."

When you move from spot to spot, change calls. Hopefully, the gobbler will think that there is yet another hen who is out looking for him. Sometimes, an aggressive hunter will change his position several times. But by moving, he often spooks the tom. Experienced hunters say that patience bags more gobblers than running and gunning.

Setting Up On A Gobbler With Hens

One of the hardest gobblers to set up on and call to is the gobbler with hens. This gobbler already has what he's looking for

A tree that is wider than your shoulders, open woods for the tom to walk through and a clear shooting lane are the essential elements to setting up for gobblers.

and is reluctant to leave his harem just to meet and mate with a new lady friend. So the first few times you call, he probably won't come. But if you continue to call, his curiosity will get the best of him. There are three tactics that the hunter can use to take this gobbler.

1. Follow the gobbler through the woods as he moves with his hens. Stay out of sight, but continue to call to the gobbler using loud, demanding calls. Often a gobbler will leave his hens or encourage his hens to walk with him to find the hunter he assumes to be another hen.

2. Most often there will be a boss hen with the gobbler and several other hens. When you start giving a demanding call, the boss hen may answer your call as if to say, "This is my gobbler. You leave him alone." That's the time to forget about trying to talk to the gobbler and instead talk directly to the boss hen. Attempt to intimidate the boss hen and cause her to become so angry that she will come over to investigate the hen that's doing all the aggressive calling to her gobbler.

When she comes hunting the caller, she'll usually bring the harem of hens with her, and the tom should accompany her. Let the boss hen walk past without seeing you. The other hens will come into the area and so will the gobbler. When you get ready to make the shot, remember that more than one set of eyes are watching for movement. Numerous gobblers have been killed by hunters who called to the boss hen and then waited for the gobbler to follow.

3. If the boss hen is ready to breed, she may answer your aggressive calling but not leave the gobbler to investigate. Then you must talk with both the hen and the gobbler. When the hen calls, call back aggressively. The instant the tom quits gobbling, start calling to him. If you want to talk to both, each time one of them calls, call back. This should excite either the hen or the gobbler. If the boss hen won't leave the gobbler, the longbeard will usually herd the boss hen over to the hunter.

Gobblers Across The Water

Another difficult turkey to set up on is the turkey that's across a body of water. Turkeys, generally, don't like to fly across water to meet a hen, and most of the time turkeys will not do so. But if there's a turkey gobbling on the other side of a creek and you prefer to avoid entering the water, there are two techniques that you can try.

If the hunter sets up in an area where the tom is accustomed to walking, the bird will not be as wary about coming in close.

1. Start calling aggressively with cuts, cackles, and excited yelping. Put some emotion in those calls. You want to make the gobbler think there's a hen that's so excited about breeding that she just can't stand it. Frequently, a gobbler will become just as excited and drum and strut in hopes of getting the hen to fly across the creek to him.

Once you've got the turkey fired up and know he can't see you, start calling and moving away from the edge of the riverbank. This will create a picture in the gobbler's mind of a hen that's ready and wanting to breed. But since the tom won't fly across the creek to meet her, she's going to walk off and locate a gobbler on her side of the water. Hopefully, the gobbler won't be able to stand the pressure of that hen walking away and will fly across the creek. Be sure to listen for the gobbler's beating wings because sometimes a longbeard will fly right to the caller.

2. If a turkey is hung up across water you must paint a picture in that gobbler's mind of a harem of hens that are excited and ready to breed. Imitate a one-man band, cutting and cackling with a diaphragm call, while yelping and cutting on a box call. Then change calls and try to sound like a whole flock of hens, each with a different voice and excited about mating. Often, a gobbler that

hears that much hen talk on the other side of a creek just can't stand the pressure. He believes that some gobbler will breed those hens in a short time and that it might just as well be himself, even if he has to fly across the creek for the date.

Setting Up On Gobblers Strutting In The Field

The gobbler strutting in the field is often the easiest turkey to find but can be the most difficult bird to set up on and call. Usually when a tom is out in the field, he either has hens with him or is in a place where hens should come. The natural order of things is that when a hen sees a gobbler, she should go to him. There are three ways to set up and take this type of tom.

1. A daylight field gobbler is a tom that flies from the roost at daylight, remains in a field all day long and then flies back to the roost at dark. He's a difficult bird to kill. However, if the hunter reaches the field before daylight and takes a stand 10 to 15 yards in the woods off the edge of the field, he can confuse a gobbler and make him come to his call. Once the hunter has taken a stand, he can begin to call to the gobbler before daylight, before the tom has started gobbling or any other hens have awakened. The hunter should begin his calling just as light is beginning to glow in the east. When the bird wakes up and hears a hen calling to him from the field before fly-down time, he wonders if there's a new hen moving into his area. He'll often fly down from the roost to meet her before the other hens wake up.

2. In the middle of the day, especially late in the season, hens will leave a gobbler by 10 a.m. to return to their nests, which leaves the gobbler all alone in the field. If the hunter takes a stand 30 to 40 yards off the field and begins calling and using light yelps, clucks and purrs, he can get the gobbler's attention and make the tom believe that there's one hen left to breed before the day is over.

3. If there are three or four gobblers in a field with a group of hens, the hunter may have a chance to take a subordinate bird. Remember that since the boss gobbler claims the right to breed the hens, subordinate toms may not have had an opportunity to breed any of the hens in the field. Therefore, if you set up fairly close to one of these subordinate gobblers that's not strutting, you may be able to call him right up to your blind.

Setting Up On Walking And Talking Gobblers

There's nothing more frustrating than to find a good gobbling bird, call to him and then listen to him walk off. In many instances these turkey are call-shy because they've listened to so much calling from other hunters that they know what a turkey call sounds like and don't want any part of it. Or maybe walking and talking gobblers just don't like hens. They'll gobble good but won't come to calling. There are two methods you can use to bag one of these walking and talking gobblers.

1. Circle the gobbler and take a stand in the woods where you think the turkey is going. Don't call to the turkey anymore and the tom should come in silently. For some people, this is a boring way to hunt, but this technique can be successful.

2. Use two hunters. The first hunter takes a stand close to where the turkey is gobbling and then calls to the tom, just enough to keep the bird gobbling. The other hunter circles the turkey, gets in front of the tom and keeps up with his location as the turkey answers the caller. This, too, will pay gobbler dividends.

Setting Up On The Hung-Up Gobbler

What should you do if a longbeard is standing 70 yards in front of you strutting, drumming and doing everything a wild turkey gobbler is supposed to do? First off, it's important to understand why a turkey hangs up out of shotgun range. Perhaps the hunter has called too much and the gobbler thinks that, "If that hen is so excited about mating, she ought to come to me when she hears me drum. I'm not going any closer to her."

Another possibility is that you're calling from a location where the tom has been shot at or attacked by a predator. Or perhaps the turkey spotted something, like movement when you sat down, the glint off the gun's barrel or a camo pattern that doesn't match the woods. A gobbler also knows that when he starts to strut he should be able to see the hen. For some reason, the tom has held up out of gun range. Here are two techniques you can try to get close enough for a shot.

1. Call to the bird with soft clucks and purrs with a different call—try a slate call rather than the mouth diaphragm. The tom, however, might still refuse to move closer.

Probably the best tactic to use is to quit calling and allow the bird to settle down. Hopefully, he'll assume that the hen has left him, and walk away. Once the tom is well out of sight, circle the bird and try to set up a calling position parallel to the direction you think the turkey went. Change calls and begin calling very softly. Since the gobbler was already fired up, it's best to call very little.

2. Let's say that a bird hangs up just out of range. You quit

calling and he walks off. Although you would like to follow him, you must get back for work. The following morning, set up closer to or actually in the area where the gobbler was strutting the day before. Since the tom thinks that the area is safe even with a hunter calling from that area, he may come in without any problem.

Setting Up Two Hunters On One Tom

One of the best reasons to hunt with a partner is that you can enjoy the natural camaraderie that results when two people pit their skills against one gobbler. For obvious safety reasons, be sure to keep visual contact with each other.

1. *The Beginner.* Something magical happens to the beginner when he sees his first strutting bird. The result, at times, is that sanity and rationality take a vacation. For that reason, it's often best to place the experienced hunter in complete control. Many like to sit against a tree and have the novice sit between their legs. This way, it's easy for the two to communicate. The experienced hunter can simply whisper or tap the beginner to inform him of the distance to the bird and when to shoot.

2. *Shooter Out Front.* If you're hunting with a veteran hunter who's planning to shoot while you call, one option is to put him 15 to 20 yards in front of you. He already knows what to look for and when to shoot—you won't have to tell him the distance. Your job will be to concentrate on calling the bird. Because the tom expects the hen to be another 20 yards away, he will be less wary as he passes the veteran hunter in search of the hen. Also, if the tom hangs up 50 yards in front of you, your partner might still be close enough for a shot.

3. *Side By Side.* One technique favored by some experienced hunting partners is to hunt side by side. Both hunters sit with their backs to the same tree. They sit close enough so they can whisper back and forth as a turkey comes near. Whichever side the turkey comes in on, that hunter gets the shot.

13

Waterfowl Decoying Strategies
by Bill Miller

Various decoys are available to the modern waterfowl hunter and the selection continues to expand. Seems like every waterfowl hunter with the slightest inclination toward invention comes up with at least one "sure fire" decoy design during his lifetime. Though the percentage of these that are ever marketed is probably minuscule, enough new designs hit the sporting goods stores every year to leave a hunter's head spinning. Some work great, some are as good as anything else out there, and some, well, they're a lot more alluring to hunters than they are to ducks and geese!

Though there can be no doubt that "high-tech" has come to waterfowl decoying, the use and deployment of decoys whether they are recycled tires, painted bleach bottles, sheets of printed plastic or custom statuettes relying on space-age components is far more important. What follows, then, are recommendations on the right decoys for the job at hand and strategies for deploying the decoys to bring ducks and geese within range of your shotgun.

The Right Decoy

Hunting with just one type of decoy may limit your waterfowling success. Even if you do the majority of your hunting in one place under relatively unchanging circumstances, you could improve your hunting success by owning several types of decoys. That way the ducks won't begin to recognize your rig. And for the hunter

Decoy Types, Recommended Uses, Advantages and Disadvantages

Decoy	Recommended Uses	Advantages	Disadvantages
Standard Size Weighted Keel	All around water hunting; especially good for secluded water with waves and/or wind	Inexpensive; compact; ride rough water better than aqua keel decoys; available in many species	Low visibility in big water; heavier than aqua keel decoys
Standard-sized Aqua Keel	All-around small water hunting; good for foot-accessible-only hunting	Inexpensive; light for easy carrying to remote hunting locations	Low visibility in big water. Do not ride rough water as well as weighted keel dekes
Magnum-weighted Keel	Best all-around size for hunting under all conditions	Good visibility on bigger waters; ride most water conditions very naturally	Bulky; heavy; difficult to transport in quantity to remote hunting sites
Magnum Aqua Keel	Good second choice if limited to secluded, sheltered waters	Good visibility on bigger waters; easier to transport in quantity	Do not ride rough waters naturally
Super Magnum Weighted Keel	Big water hunting applications such as reservoir, tidal flat and ocean hunting	Best visibility in all conditions; long-range drawing power	Heavy, cumbersome, expensive; special arrangements necessary to transport large spread
Standard Shell	General field hunting with large spread	Extremely lifelike; stackable for easy storage and transport	Low visibility especially against broken background
Magnum Shell	Good size for general field hunting	Extremely lifelike; stackable for easy storage and transport	Expensive, bulky
Super Magnum Shell	Best size for field hunting	Extremely lifelike; fewer decoys needed for same drawing power as spread of standards or magnums	Cost prohibitive for big spreads; impractical for transport to remote hunting areas
Windsocks	General field hunting; especially good for combining with shell and/or rag decoys	Impart motion to spread and can be set up quickly; self-adjust to wind shifts	Expensive, maintenance-intensive because of weak wooden/plastic components
Rag Decoys	Field hunting with large spreads; good in combination with shells and/or windsocks	Quick to deploy and pick up; low cost and weight make huge spreads possible in remote hunting locations	No height; tend to blow around in moderate to strong winds

Others—see "Specialty Decoys" section of this chapter

who hunts a number of areas under a variety of conditions, owning the right decoy spread for each situation is critical to success.

For example, say on opening day you want to avoid the crowds at the popular, boat-accessible public hunting areas. Instead you get out and do some early season research and locate a beaver pond on national forest land that is just loaded with wood ducks and some teal. The pond is surrounded by cedar swamp, but with a careful approach you'll be able to pitch out a few decoys near the beaver dam and have a great shoot. Rover's as primed and ready to go as you are, so there's not much worry about knocking ducks down over the deep part of the pond.

By following the hiking trails about a mile and a half from where you park the car, you'll only have to trek through a couple hundred yards of thick cedar bog. Even though the limit's three ducks, you better take a box of shells because opening day always showcases too little off season practice. Then you'll need calls and a thermos of coffee. You can either wear your waders if it's cool or carry them and put 'em on before you hit the cedars. Won't do much good to go without a gun. And Rover has been doing so well that it would be a shame to not take the camera along.

Well, for one afternoon's shoot, that ought to be enough gear. You've got everything except the decoys. Imagine the drudgery of carrying a dozen weighted keel magnums along with all that other gear out to the beaver pond and back! Might make you think about going grouse hunting instead.

This is the perfect situation for a dozen standard-sized water keel decoys. Better yet, the new collapsible kind that compact in your pack, then "inflate" when tossed onto the pond. The pond is so sheltered by the cedar swamp that wind should have little effect on the spread, and ducks that go far off the beaten path should be "green" to hunters so early in the year. They won't be looking over the spread nearly as closely as they will a few days into the season.

The situation is the same for the goose hunter who gets permission to hunt a huge feeding field as long as he agrees not to dig pits or drive on the field. Carrying sacks of full-bodied decoys over muddy croplands is asking for a coronary. Rag decoys and lightweight shells were made for times when you've got to walk a long way to set up the spread.

On the other hand, late season geese that are wary of lighting with real live birds might not even land in the same county with such a simple spread. That's when professional guides in heavily hunted country like Maryland's Eastern Shore bring out specially built trailers full of "stuffers"—actual taxidermied geese used as decoys. How's that for taking the theory of the right decoy for the job to the extreme?

Of course, economics puts a limit on how many decoys and how many types of decoys most waterfowl hunters can own. With that in mind, consider various waterfowl decoys along with recommended uses and advantages and disadvantages for each. You should look at the recommended uses for each carefully and match them to the kind of hunting you do most often. Start building your personal collection there.

Motion—A Critical Element

One sob story that is shared by waterfowlers everywhere is the tale of the flock that always comes out of nowhere just as you have your boat about halfway out to pick up the first decoy. It seems to happen to every hunter at least once a season, and to some a lot more than that.

A classic example occurred while shooting an episode of "Celebrity Outdoors" for The Nashville Network (TNN) cable television network. We were hunting with the Blue Goose Hunting Club near Eagle Lake, Texas. The celebrities in our group consisted of Little Jimmy Dickens and Charlie Walker of the Grand Ol' Opry, but also along were three extra guns (of which the author was one), two camera/sound men, the producer and five of Blue Goose's most experienced guides.

Besides the size of our group, we had a bunch of other elements working against us. First, we were hunting in early January which is near the end of the Texas waterfowl season. That meant these birds had already been hunted for almost five months as they migrated and for more than two months in the very fields we were hunting them. These late-season Texas geese are the survivors who have seen every trick in the book and lived to tell about them.

Second, the schedule for shooting was such that we only had one morning to get the goose hunting portion of the show in the can. During our brief visit, we also needed to tape a pheasant hunting segment and a sporting clays segment, so it was do or die on the geese that morning.

Finally, the point of the show was to have these old-time celebrities hunting and taking snow geese in the old-time ways— wearing white parkas and laying among a huge spread of rag decoys in a Texas rice field. That in itself didn't cause any problems, but when the morning dawned the weather was clear and warm with little wind. We knew that we had a tough job on our hands. "Bluebird weather" is the toughest kind in which to pull birds with a rag spread and hunters in whites.

Normally, when faced with such conditions, Texas goose guides will suggest their hunters strip down to camouflage clothing and then move to a ditch or fence row several hundred yards downwind of the spread. Usually, the wary birds will flare a good distance from the decoys, but offer decent pass shooting to the hidden hunters. However, because of what this show was trying to portray, such tactics were not an option.

As usually happens on such Texas hunts, our group limited out on white-fronted geese and Canada geese in the first hour of the hunt, but the wary snows and blues eluded us. Even flocks that gave us a look-see flared hundreds of yards away—not because we were doing anything wrong, but because the late-season birds are just that wary.

Later in the day, we watched flocks circle for 15 minutes before landing in a field of more than 3,000 real feeding geese! Some flocks even flared from the huge congregation of real birds and never did land in that field!

But anyone who happened to catch that episode of "Celebrity Outdoors" will say, "Hey, I saw you guys take snow geese on that show! What gives?"

Indeed, we did take eight snows and blues on that morning's hunt. Two were singles that did come within range. The other six came from a flock that decoyed after we were "finished" hunting.

When we suspected that we'd get no more birds that morning, we unloaded our guns and gathered together near the center of the 1,500 decoy spread to tape the "set-up" shots that are part of any outdoors shows. Such things as interviews in the field, close-ups of guides calling and low-angle shots of dogs retrieving are all normally taken either before or after the actual hunting footage.

So with almost a dozen people standing up in the decoys, two dogs running around, the uncovered camera elevated on a tripod and nobody really paying much attention to anything but the taping, a flock of better than 50 snows and blues decided to come right on in. Those of us close enough to our unloaded guns dove for them and fumbled to drop some shells into the chambers. Following the wild melee we managed to knock six light geese from the flock that flew unconcernedly into our midst.

Snow geese can be the easiest or the toughest waterfowl to decoy. It all depends upon hunting pressure and weather.

Naturally, the topic of discussion for the rest of the trip was devoted to determining why those birds came in when all the others had refused our best efforts at staying hidden among the rags and windsocks.

The most logical answer is motion. We surely couldn't have looked a great deal like geese, but from the distance that the flock first spotted us (probably well over a mile), the exaggerated motion of a dozen men moving around in the decoys added an attraction factor we had been missing the rest of the morning.

Face it, whether in a feeding field or resting on the water, ducks and geese don't plop out of the sky and become statues. When feeding or lounging, ducks and geese are a blur of motion! They fight for choice morsels, they preen, they look around for danger, they tip up to feed and they stretch their wings. Unless they are asleep, they are never really still.

The serious, observant waterfowler will quickly recognize that he is fighting a losing battle when he tries to set up a realistic looking spread using only traditional, non-moving decoys. Even if every feather of your decoy spread is carved in the finest detail, you won't be able to achieve ultimate realism until you put movement into the spread.

Next to the seductive calling of a well-trained "Suzy," movement was the reason that live decoys were outlawed for hunting in North America. What more realistic movement could be possible than a flock of real birds?

Adding movement to your waterfowl decoy spread isn't difficult. You simply need to analyze the type of movement necessary to make your decoy spread look like a flock of real birds. Often, that which nature already provides will give a spread lifelike movement.

For example, on open water or in an open field, the wind will give some types of decoys lifelike movement. Floating puddle duck decoys, properly tethered with the anchor line running through the front hole on the keel will appear to swim somewhat in gusting winds, yet keep the spread oriented facing upwind which is natural for waterfowl.

Wind is relied upon in the design of some field decoys like wind socks. Even a slight breeze will billow out these decoys and orient them into the breeze. Fluctuations in the wind flow give them alluring, lifelike movement. The "Farm Form" decoy which is a cone shaped variation of the traditional full-bodied decoy uses the wind to produce a very realistic waddle. Though they don't actually move forward, when viewed from a distance a spread of

Farm Forms looks like a flock of real geese waddling into the wind as they feed in harvested grain fields. Wind even adds a lifelike ripple to traditional rag decoys or their modern variants like the Texas Hunting Products Sheet-Dec.

Obviously, wind is relied upon to provide movement to decoys in open water diver and sea duck hunting. Several strings of bluebill decoys popping over the waves can appear very realistic as long as the right decoys are chosen for the conditions. Heavy waves require solid, properly balanced and keeled decoys to present a realistic look on the water. As these species receive greater gunning pressure because of the current decline in puddle duck species' populations, divers and sea ducks won't continue to be fooled by decoys which don't ride the waves like the real thing.

Unfortunately, the wind is a fickle thing. If you're counting on it to provide all of the lifelike motion in your decoy spread, you probably won't have it when you need it most. Several situations in puddle duck hunting almost preclude the use of wind for lifelike movement.

For example, flooded timber hunting and hunting small, woodland potholes or sloughs hide you and the ducks from the wind. That's what often makes those types of places alluring to hunters and ducks.

Arkansas probably is most famous for flooded timber hunting, and there duck hunting guides have been imparting motion to their decoys for years simply by splashing around in the water.

Successful timber hunters rely more upon their setup to sound like real birds than look realistic because by the time a flock of real birds actually sees the decoys, they are already pretty much committed. That's why big, loud calling plays such an important role in a lot of flooded timber hunting.

However, one of timber hunting's subtleties is to splash the surface of the water with your hand, foot or paddle. Not only does this make sounds like a bunch of mallards splashing and feeding beneath the timber canopy, but it also creates radiating rings of surface disturbance like that caused by real ducks. While the anchored decoys stay in one place, these rings radiate out around the spread, catching the light as they move below the openings in the treetops. Ducks that might otherwise miss the location of the spread completely because of the density of the timber, can hone in on the source of these wavelets. Those moving, concentric ripples will be found wherever ducks are active on the water and appear entirely natural to the flying ducks.

When you're hunting a small pond or slough, or anytime the wind isn't helping to move the decoys, you can add movement by creating these wave rings. The system can be as simple as carrying a pocketful of stones to your hunting area and flipping them out into the decoys when an interested flock's attention is focused elsewhere. It doesn't sound very sophisticated, and it isn't—but it does work. The drawbacks are getting caught throwing at the wrong time, making sure Rover knows you're not practicing retrieving and taking the chance that any uninitiated hunters will tell stories back at the club about the nut who was chuckin' rocks at his own decoys!

Another way to create this kind of wave action in your decoys is to set up your own simple, splasher decoy system.

After all the other decoys are set, run an 80-foot length of dark-colored cord with a small snap on one end through the eye of some kind of anchor weighing a pound or better. Lock the dull-finished snap in place on the anchor line hole on the keel of a flip-tail feeder style of decoy. With the decoy in one hand, and the spool of cord in the other, lower the anchor slowly to the bottom while trying to avoid tangling the line in any weeds.

Plop the decoy gently on the water over the anchor and slowly back away from the decoy toward your blind while allowing the necessary length of cord to roll off the spool.

Test the splasher by pulling gently on the cord to see that it creates an up-and-down motion on the flip-tail and isn't tangled in the weeds. Then, slowly move toward your blind. Be careful that the cord doesn't foul in any of the anchor lines holding decoys you've already set.

From the blind you'll be able to jiggle and bounce that flip-tail feeder like a real duck scrounging below the surface.

You can make this system as elaborate as you like by incorporating more splashers in the spread or by creating a custom splasher like a full-bodied decoy which actually can sit on the water or tip up like a flip-tail feeder.

One more hint is to have the blind end of the cord actually attached to the spool and make the spool of something that floats. Then, even if the spool is dropped in the excitement of calling and shooting, it can be found quickly and the anchor won't be lost.

The range at which ducks will pick up on this kind of decoy motion and wave action is amazing, but it is particularly effective in convincing those maddening birds that seem to circle forever just out of range. In cold weather a splasher system will also keep

Splasher Rig

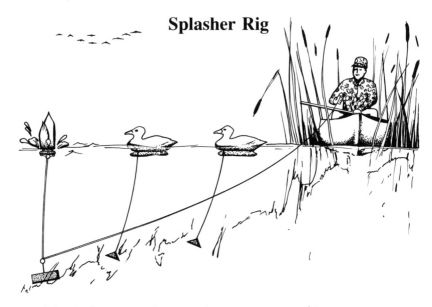

One of the simplest ways to impart motion to a water spread is to create your own splasher rig with a decoy, a heavy anchor and a good length stout cord.

ice from forming in your spread. Fairly regular motion postpones icing for several hours depending upon the conditions.

A variety of motorized decoys are available to add motion to the spread as well. Some simply use a propeller to create the same kind of motion as the splasher rig while anchored in one spot. There are also elaborate radio-controlled models that will swim throughout the rig under your control. The most sophisticated of these even have tongs on the front for the dogless hunter to use in retrieving birds that are killed outright in range of the remote control decoy. Obviously cost is a major consideration on motorized decoys with prices ranging from about $50 for the simplest motorized splasher up to several hundred dollars for a radio controlled decoy.

Another type of motion that traditional decoys fail to produce is the wing stretching which waterfowl seem to do constantly. Watch a large flock of ducks or geese on the water or in a field and you'll almost never spend more than a few seconds without seeing one or more birds in the flock extend and then refold their wings. In human terms, it must be like scratching one's head or tying a shoe.

Wing stretching is a motion that can be seen for quite adistance. In fact, it probably extends the range at which a flock of flying birds can pick up on another flock already feeding. By adding this natural sort of motion to a decoy spread, its drawing range is also likely to be increased.

Imitation of wing-stretching is what generated the decoying technique known as flagging which originated with the commercial goose hunting operations on the eastern coast of the United States, particularly on Maryland's eastern shore. Canada geese migrating through and wintering in this area are hunted hard and become spread-shy quickly. Commercial hunting operations in this area use every legal technique they can to bring in birds for their hunters. The extremes they go to include flocks of "stuffers"—actual taxidermied geese used as decoys.

Even with such extravagant realism at their disposal, the key element of motion was missing. That's how flagging came about.

Flagging or winging on the most basic level is simply waving a pair of flags or paddles to attract the attention of distant birds. For Canada geese the flags are usually black or dark gray.

Flagging techniques can be as varied as the hunters performing this waterfowler's semaphore. Some guides only flag until a distant flock has been turned toward the spread. Others have had great success flagging the birds right into shotgun range. Some say the flagging should only be done at ground level, just above the edge of a pit blind in the middle of the decoys. Others will stand up and flag from the edge of the decoy spread. Some will stand tall and flag above their heads until the birds are coming in, then slowly lower the flapping paddles until they are crouching and the paddles are moving just above the ground.

What all this means is that developing your own successful flagging techniques will be a trial-and-error proposition, but well worth the time when you find the right code.

It seems, too, that techniques like flagging work not only because they imitate a natural movement of the birds, but because waterfowl have an innate curiosity about movements they don't understand. In reality, this is probably the reason those ducks come in when you are in the boat picking up decoys or why those snow geese finally decoyed when our whole television crew was milling around the rag spread.

Hunters in the Maritime Provinces of Canada have exploited this waterfowl curiosity for years with a unique hunting technique. The story goes that a market hunter was having a poor day gunning the shores of Nova Scotia. Birds were present, but none would come within range of his gun.

As with all hunters, his attention wandered during the lulls in

The technique of flagging geese probably works for two reasons. The moving flags are a rough imitation of a goose's wing stretching motions and waterfowl seem to have an innate curiosity about motion they don't immediately recognize as danger.

shooting. During one such slow stretch he noticed a pair of red foxes coming up the shoreline. The foxes spotted a raft of ducks some distance offshore. When they did, one fox crouched in the rocks in shallow water while the second began to parade back and forth on the beach.

It wasn't long before the raft of ducks was paddling shoreward, apparently hypnotized by the fox they could see running back and forth on the beach. As the ducks came closer and closer to shore, the showman fox moved farther and farther back on the shore and carried on his maneuvers.

The hidden fox crouched lower in the water. Soon there were ducks swimming all around him, and it wasn't long before one swam too close to his lightning-fast jaws. In a split second the hidden fox had a duck and a meal for him and his partner.

The incident started those inventive wheels turning in the market hunter's mind, and it wasn't long until he decided that he could train his small reddish-yellow and white retriever to behave just as the prancing fox had. He would lay in wait like the hidden fox and shoot at the rafts of ducks on the water as market gunners have done without compunction.

The result we know today is a breed of dog called the Nova Scotia Tolling Retriever and a method of hunting called tolling. Tolling with dogs is still done today in Canada's eastern provinces, modified of course to take the birds on the wing. Every waterfowl hunter who longs to experience all the types of duck and goose hunting North America has to offer must include a hunt in Nova Scotia, New Brunswick or Prince Edward Island with an outfitter who tolls ducks with a dog. There is no other hunting experience like it anywhere.

The only explanation why tolling, or to some extent flagging, works is that waterfowl have a natural level of curiosity. Until they recognize that a particular kind of motion means danger, they won't react negatively to it. In fact, as tolling with dogs and poling the canoe among the decoys prove, they'll often come to investigate.

Another way to impart wing-stretching appearance to a decoy rig is to incorporate some of the new wing attachments into your spread. These are simply sets of plastic wings which clip onto the backs of standard floating or field decoys. Though they don't actually move, having several sets of outstretched wings spread out around the rig definitely adds realism.

In a field spread, it is a great idea to prop up the birds you kill as additional decoys. If you don't already have wings on any of your field dekes, go ahead and spread the wings of your harvested birds to add that desirable touch of life.

As much as movement among the decoys is lifelike and alluring, metallic flashing or bright reflection will send birds flaring faster than anything. In developing schemes to incorporate motion into your spread, avoid metallic finishes.

For example, even white is not white in a snow goose spread. It's the reason dull finished white plastic rags like Texas Hunting Products Sheet-Decs work on sunny days when plain old, shiny finished white kitchen trash bags will flare birds like an animal-rights fanatic using a bull horn. Real geese don't glint in the sun.

Shine a bright flashlight on a brand new cloth diaper, then shine it on the polished door of a smooth finished, white refrigerator —that's the same difference in dull white and shiny white that the birds will see from the air as they cruise overhead.

The one possible exception to flash as a repellent to waterfowl may be the muted reflection of the metallic speculum on duck's wings. Going back to the attracting abilities of the wing stretch, a bright speculum flashing in the sun may have some allure to waterfowl; however, it seems more likely that the actual attention-getting mechanism is the light underside of the wings and breast which are revealed when a duck stretches its wings.

Some innovators have recommended that prismatic tape be placed over the painted speculum on duck decoys, but no conclusive results have been proven. Seeing two-dozen pieces of metallic tape flashing in the sun tends to sap the confidence of hardcore waterfowlers who fight shiny ice buildup on decoys season after season. Therefore, it may be some time before reflective speculums on decoys get a fair and conclusive testing.

Decoying On A New Plane

If you're like most waterfowl hunters once you've added lifelike motion to your decoy spreads, you'll step back and take a look at your handiwork. Go ahead: Pat yourself on the back for your innovation and dedication, but soon you'll be asking the next logical question, "Now what will make this even better?"

One good answer is, "Depth!" Yes, depth.

Traditional water and field decoy spreads are very two dimensional. They encompass length and width alright, but most have very little height.

On the most subtle level, traditional field and floating decoys sit very low to the ground. Some designs of floating mallard decoys have no necks at all. Both the drakes and the hens have the head nestled right down on the body like a resting duck. That's fine for part of the spread, but seldom are all the ducks in a flock resting at the same time.

Goose decoys tend to be more three dimensional because of the birds' long necks, but even beginning hunters know that in a goose spread you should have no more than one sentinel neck to every three or four feeder heads. Otherwise, your spread mimics a flock of spooked birds, and that is far less alluring to wary geese than a contentedly feeding flock of feathered brethren.

The problem with traditional field goose decoys is that most are designed to have the flat underside of the shell sit right down on the ground. That makes a spread look like a field full of birds sitting on nests; again, not very natural.

The answer is to throw in some of the new full-bodied shell decoys complete with breasts, legs and feet. Flambeau, Big Foot, Carry-Lite and other companies are manufacturing these most lifelike of all molded plastic goose decoys. G&H Decoys is making detachable goose feet which can be added right in the field to standard field-shell decoys. A hunter with an imaginative eye can spread these throughout a field rig with a sentinel head here, a few tilted bodies with feeder heads there, and add a tremendous boost of realism.

Viewed from almost any range, getting a few decoys up on their feet really takes a field spread from good to great. But doing so only takes the spread from a foot and a half in depth to perhaps three and a half feet. A lot more can be done to take decoying farther into the third dimension. Namely, the addition of flying decoys!

Two types of flying decoys are available to the modern waterfowl hunter. The most versatile type is a full-bodied molded plastic decoy in the shape of a flying duck or goose. They come with detachable wings for more compact storage and transport, but when assembled look exactly like a landing bird. These are suspended on camouflaged metal or fiberglass poles stuck in the ground or marsh bottom. If several are used they are generally placed just down wind of the intended landing area in the decoys. For the most realistic effect, the front bird in the V is best located just above the water or stubble while the back birds may be as high as 12 or 15 feet in the air. The new heights to which you take your spread depends upon how much conduit you're willing to tote out to your hunting area.

Along these same lines, Feather Flex offers what it calls "Wingers." These are top-view silhouettes of flying ducks and geese that are placed on poles like the full-bodied flying decoys. Waterfowl flying overhead see these as birds flying at a lower altitude; however, when viewed in profile from the lower angle of a decoying bird, Wingers tend to disappear. Wingers are much lighter, more compact and far less expensive than the full-bodied decoys.

Another type of flying full-bodied decoy are wind socks with wings. Northwind Decoys, for example, offers a windsock that billows into the shape of a flying goose when the wind fills it. These, too, can be suspended on poles of varying heights and offer the advantage of self-adjustment to changing wind directions. Keeping flying decoys looking like they are landing into the wind

Cabela's and other mail-order sporting goods companies offer lifelike full-bodied flying decoys that appear to hover over a spread when positioned atop conduit poles.

is a critical element in maintaining realism. Birds do not land with the wind!

The other major type of flying decoys are kites designed to look like flying geese. These are often used in conjunction with rag spreads for snow geese and by sophisticated commercial Canada goose hunting operations. When combined with a large, well-set field spread, kites can be deadly on all types of geese. They offer the advantage of being light and compact, yet allow you to set flying decoys at heights much greater than it is practical to place full-bodied decoys on poles.

Besides creating a three-dimensional appearance to the spread, kite decoys can be used as great range and elevation markers for taking incoming birds. Texas guides sometimes set a decoy for a first-time hunter and tell him not to shoot unless the bird is closer than the kite. It really helps reduce the number of shots an inexperienced hunter takes at birds still out of range.

Goose kites, like these from Farm Form Decoys, are ideal "third dimension" attractants when conditions are right.

Until you've tried hunting with kites, you can't imagine how realistic they look in the air, but you'll quickly learn. Even experienced kite flyers will sometimes catch a glimpse of the flying fake out of the corner of an eye and quickly roll into shooting position only to see their own decoy floating over the shotgun's front bead!

Of course, the kite decoy's major disadvantage is its reliance upon wind. A good steady breeze is needed to keep the kite aloft, and such is often lacking on foggy, rainy days when the birds seem to be most easily decoyed.

Rigging Decoys For Realism And Convenience

The most common way to rig floating decoys for shallow water hunting is to simply tie an anchor cord to the front eyelet on the keel of the decoy. The other end of the cord is then attached to an anchor of appropriate weight. This is a simple and straight forward system, but it can be improved with some thought.

Shallow-water decoy rigs frequently are set or picked up in the dark. Making the procedure as simple and "snag free" as possible will cut down on the time it takes to lay the spread and allow you more time to savor some more of that once-delicious warm coffee during those magic, pre-dawn moments in the blind.

Snag-free rigging of shallow water decoys is really done at home and relies on consistency. It is critical that every decoy in the spread be rigged identically! That way the procedure for deploying or collecting the rig will become second nature. With a little experience your hands will know just where to reach for each step in the process. You will literally be able to set the spread with your eyes closed!

A great way to rig shallow-water decoys is to tie the anchor line to the front hole on the keel. Then loop a heavy-duty rubber band into the hole at the back of the keel. Before cutting the anchor line, do several wraps around the keel to the approximate length which you want the anchor line. Four to 7 feet is usually sufficient depending upon the area you'll be hunting.

Estimate so the end of the anchor line falls just short of the unstretched rubber band, then cut it at that point. Tie the largest, dull-finished fishing snap swivel you can find to the end of the anchor line and hook it through the rubber band loop. That's one decoy done.

With this kind of rig the anchors are placed in a separate little bag which can be thrown into the decoy bag along with the blocks. Then when you arrive at the hunting area, lay out the anchors on the boat seat in front of you, pull a decoy from the bag, unhook the snap swivel, lock an anchor in place, unwrap the line and place the decoy. When picking up the spread, reverse the process and rebag the anchors in their own storage container.

Though it may sound tedious, it's really not once the decoys are rigged. The system eliminates tangles because the wound line is always snugged by the elasticity of the rubber band. Also, transporting and storing the decoys without anchors attached prolongs the life of the paint on the decoy. Indeed, there are other methods nearly as tangleproof, but all of them leave a lot of lead bouncing around in the bag with the decoys. If one of these methods is used, be sure to secure the anchors tightly at the keel, not around the head, neck or tail of the decoy. Anchor line looped around the body and bendable lead anchors secured around a decoy's neck will quickly scrape away a realistic paint job.

Rigging large numbers of decoys for quick deployment in deep, open water is another ball game entirely. Where a shallow-water puddle duck spread might normally range from six to 50 dekes, open-water hunting for divers or sea ducks might call for several hundred decoys.

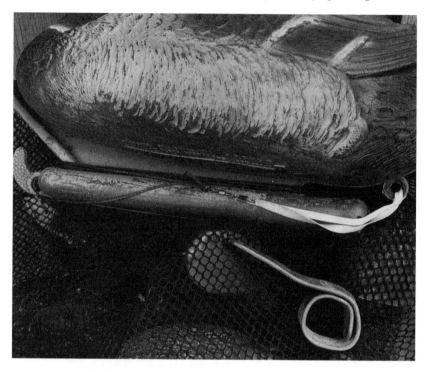

When rigged in this manner, the rubber band snugs the anchor line in place to avoid frustrating tangles. The anchors are stored separately to avoid chipping the paint on the decoys.

Deep-water rigging of large numbers of decoys is another area of waterfowling in which nearly every hunter has tried to let his ingenuity show through. Unfortunately, systems which reduce the potential for tangling are often cumbersome and not very convenient, especially for the modern waterfowler who relies on mobility for success.

Drew Ursin is a technical adviser for Beretta U.S.A and a registered hunting guide in Maryland, but he doesn't claim to be anything more than a good ol' boy with a little bit of common sense. Well, that sure shows through in the way Drew rigs his decoys for sea-duck hunting. The system is called a daisy chain.

About seven to 15 scoter or eider decoys are strung together by attaching heavy, dark-colored decoy line from the back eye on the keel of one decoy to the front eye of the decoy behind it in the chain. The distance between the decoys is about 4 to 6 feet.

To the front eye of the lead decoy in the chain is attached the

Daisy Chain

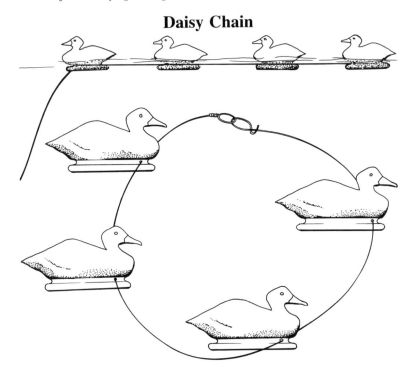

The daisy chain system is convenient for rigging large numbers of decoys which will be deployed in string formations on large bodies of open water.

main anchor line which may be 80 or more feet long, depending upon the depth of the water and the wave conditions in which you'll likely be hunting. To the other end of this line is attached a substantial anchor like a window-sash weight. The anchor line is then wound around this weight for storage.

The decoys themselves are strung onto an opened clothes hanger or, better yet, an appropriate length of smooth bailing wire. Always put the lead decoy on the chain first, following with each successive decoy in order. The wire should slide through the front eye of each decoy. When all decoys are strung into place, tie the wire off into a circle. The decoys pointing outward from the circle give the appearance of a flower blossom, thus the name "daisy" chain emerges.

At his hunting location, Drew will slow the boat and a hunter along each rail will grab a chain of decoys and open the wire loop. As the boat moves slowly into the wind, the decoys will be dropped off the wire one by one until the strings are trailing full length off the stern and the entire main anchor line is unwound from the anchor. At just the right moment, Drew signals the hunters to drop the anchors and circles back to unwind and drop off two more lines. The system is simple and allows Drew to quickly set up a good-sized rig even with an inexperienced crew.

The crucial time in avoiding tangles is when retrieving decoys rigged on a daisy chain. Because the approach will again be from downwind, the first decoy picked up will be from the tail of the chain and the tendency will be to start stringing blocks on the wire from that point.

As you can see, quick deployment relies on dropping the last decoy in the line first, so gather all the decoys into the boat first and begin stringing with the lead decoy.

The daisy chain system works well for diver hunting, too, when combined with clusters of singly rigged blocks or decoys rigged on spreaders.

Specialty Decoys

Besides the basic floating and field decoys and the moving and flying decoys already discussed, a few specialty additions lend even additional lifelike appearance to a decoy spread.

The most common specialty decoys are "confidence decoys." They can be replicas of any species other than those which you're after. Common ones include coot, herons, seagulls and egrets.

Confidence decoys are placed in the general vicinity of the spread to assure incoming ducks or geese that everything is alright. The distance from the spread varies depending upon the species of confidence decoy you're using. For example, heron decoys are sometimes placed 100 yards or so from the blind to assure working ducks everything is copacetic. Seagull decoys are even placed right on top of a well-camouflaged blind. A half-dozen coot placed at the far edge of shotgun range serve as a natural-looking range indicator and tend to keep ducks headed for the landing opening you've wisely positioned much closer to your blind.

Because of the herons' large size and the light coloration of seagulls, replicas of these species are more easily spotted by distant ducks and geese than small, drably colored duck decoys.

The critical element in selecting confidence decoys to add to your spread is choosing a species which is common to the area you're hunting. The wrong confidence decoy is worse than none at all because it acts as a signal to already wary birds that something

Coot are common to marshes across the continent. Having a few fakes near your main decoy spread makes the whole scene look more natural.

is out of place, and that they should keep going.

Specialty decoys should also be incorporated right into a duck or goose spread to enhance lifelike appearance. The little details, such as decoys with movable heads, spell the difference when dealing with wary ducks. The only time ducks all look in the same direction is when something has spooked them.

Spend any time at all watching ducks and geese on the water or feeding in fields and you'll quickly see that no two birds in the flock are doing exactly the same thing at the same time. Yet waterfowlers go into the field every year to try to lure wizened birds with a dozen decoys that are all doing exactly the same thing. It just doesn't make sense.

The most lifelike spread will include decoys in a variety of positions. Feeding heads, resting heads, sleeping postures, flip-tail feeders and any other natural postures should be incorporated into the spread. No one manufacturer offers all the poses, so you'll have to do some shopping. If you really want to get serious, consider building your own custom dekes based upon your own observation of ducks and geese.

Even birds of the same species don't all look exactly alike in a flock. Some are large; some are smaller. Some are dark; some are lighter. Especially in the fall, many birds still wear dull, juvenile plumage. You can achieve the same effect by mixing brands and, to some extent, sizes of decoys.

Opinions are mixed on whether super-magnum decoys and standard-sized dekes should be randomly interspersed through the spread. We're told the reason magnum decoys work is because ducks and geese do not recognize them as oversized. While waterfowl eyesight and color acuity are estimated at least 10 times better than humans, their depth perception is poor. In short, when they see a magnum decoy, they perceive it simply as a fellow fowl which is closer than it really is.

If this is indeed the case, then mixing drastically different sized decoys in the same part of the spread may be confusing and appear unnatural to ducks. Because you want to make the ducks and geese believe they understand completely what's going on below them, this could be detrimental to the effectiveness of the spread.

United But Separate

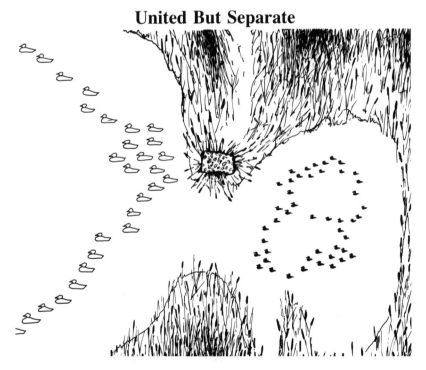

Standard and super magnum blocks can be used in the same spread; however, they are best segregated to take advantage of their full potential.

A mix of standard and huge decoys can be used in the same spread, but the giant decoys should be segregated from the smallest blocks. The best example of this would be hunting the inlet to a small bay.

With your blind positioned at the narrowest spot on the channel so you can shoot both over the open water and the bay, position the super mags on the open water and the standard-sized blocks in the bay. This way, you'll be using the long-range attracting power of the super mags and the close-range realism of the standard blocks more efficiently.

In areas where duck species are mixed, it may be wise to use several species of decoys, too. Though a number of species of ducks may use an area, you'll likely see very few truly mixed flocks. The adage "birds of a feather flock together" has its roots much deeper in reality than myth. This should tell you that in setting the spread, segregate the species as well as the sizes.

Geese will also segregate in the same feeding field, and it's amazing to see how the birds will decoy to their own kind in a spread. On a hunt in Manitoba involving NAHC President Steve Burke, Advertising Director Russ Nolan, NAHC Member Larry Schroeder and me, we were hunting from a spread of about 1,200 decoys. The shape of the spread was a rough horseshoe with the closed end downwind.

About 1,100 of the decoys were snow and blue goose rags, windsocks and shells. Obviously, they formed the vast majority of the horseshoe. About 100 dark goose shells and rags were set in a pod of their own just off to one side of the closed end of the "U."

All of the light geese we worked that morning obliged us by heading right for the opening in the middle of the spread. Then we spotted a flock of Canadas in the distance and called hard to get their attention. On this morning they were extra cautious and swung half-mile circles around the spread. In the meantime, several light geese landed amid the decoys.

The Canadas were low now, but still swinging wide of the spread. Finally they turned and flew straight away downwind—and kept going. We all half sat up, looked at each other and shrugged. Then the two hunters closest to the landed geese jumped up, hollered, flushed the birds and took them cleanly.

I was about halfway back from retrieving those geese when I heard Steve give the whisper/yell that waterfowl hunters know so well, "Get down!" He didn't have to say it twice.

I dropped with my face in the stubble and tried in vain with my gloved hand to load a third shell into my old Remington 870. A second later I heard, "take 'em".

I rolled over, mounted the gun and looked at dark geese everywhere.

I think my first shot went off before the gun was even to my shoulder, but as I pulled on a bird with my second and last, another goose crossed above it and two geese folded at the shot.

Russ had been lying closest to the dark rags, and the returning flock of Canadas almost landed on him. They had come back skimming the prairie below the horizon, locked onto that small cluster of dark goose rags. I really think they could have cared less about the 1,100 gleaming white decoys that covered better than an acre! Likewise, we probably could have decoyed all the light geese we wanted without the dark dekes at all.

United but separate rules as the motto for species and sizes of decoys for waterfowl.

What Can You Learn From Watching Waterfowl?

To perfect calling technique and to learn more about decoying, it is important to watch live ducks and geese as often as and under as many conditions as possible. How waterfowl call and how they act when undisturbed reveal keys the hunter can use to successfully lure more birds into range.

When watching flocks rest and feed, don't look so intently for the trees that you lose sight of the forest. Try to take in everything that is going on while the birds are on the ground or water and as more birds come in and leave. An avid waterfowl watcher can fill up reams of paper taking good notes of waterfowl behavior which he or she can later extrapolate into good decoying information.

For example, some observers get so intent on looking for patterns to follow in setting out decoys that they fail to notice what part of a pond or field the birds use. Or one might concentrate so intently on "poses" the birds take that he fails to notice that the birds in the flock are moving all the time.

Get out there and watch ducks and geese to learn what looks natural. Watch carefully, but do it with an open mind so you don't miss anything. The birds are the best teachers if you are willing to be a student.

Because the NAHC headquarters overlooks a wildlife management area featuring a couple of large beaver ponds, employees have found that a favorite diversion from the workday is turning away from the desk to watch the ducks and geese which visit the

In Texas geese are only hunted in the morning. That makes afternoons the perfect time to watch birds in the field to pick up pointers on improving your decoying strategies.

area at all times of the year. Most educational time is the fall because that's when the birds are in the behavior patterns which a hunter will encounter in the field.

A typical autumn will see bluewing and greenwing teal, wood ducks, wigeon, mallards, blue bills, buffleheads, mergansers and often other species on the ponds over a three- to four-week period. After a few days of viewing, it becomes quickly evident that even though all of these species are sharing the same small area, they do not mingle much. As the birds fly from pond to pond and to and from feeding grounds, rarely will they be in a mixed flock. Mallards stick with mallards, wood ducks with wood ducks, wigeon with wigeon. It's obvious how that can affect decoy placement.

When observing waterfowl, note carefully the weather and wind conditions. The common belief is that ducks decoy more easily on cloudy, foggy days, but personal observation of ducks and geese may change your opinion. Notes from watching the ducks out the NAHC windows show that in many cases, flocks usually circle more times before pitching in on dark days. Why?

Of course, only the ducks know for sure, but perhaps it has something to do with being able to pick out shiny speculums and glossy green heads more easily on sunny days. That's something to think about when selecting and positioning decoys.

Ten General Field Tips

And then there are the hints from other waterfowlers and ideas that we've stumbled on ourselves that were there all the time but were just overlooked. Here, then, are 10 quick decoying tips that should make days in the duck blind or goose field more productive and enjoyable.

1. Lead decoy anchors are shiny when they come out of the package. That's bad news when you tie a new one onto a decoy used for hunting in shallow, clear water. NAHC Member and Texas Hunting Products President Chuck Barry of Houston recommends buying the anchors at close-out sales after the hunting season and then hanging them individually on nails driven into the back fence. By the time you need them for the next fall's hunting, they'll have a nice, dull finish.

2. Owner of the Wild Goose Hunting Club and renowned guide Pat Johnson of El Campo, Texas, saves himself the back-breaking work of picking up rag decoys through the clever use of a dowel rod from one of his windsocks. Use the dowel as you move through the spread to hook and lift the rags. With a little practice you'll be able to deftly deposit the rags right into a decoy bag. This simple little trick really speeds up retrieving a huge rag spread and makes it a lot less tiring!

3. Before that crucial opening day, try to get your dog out and work him in a decoy spread. Young dogs in particular need a refresher on what decoys and anchor lines are all about. When setting decoy spreads that are rigged on long strings, consider the paths your dog will likely use to make his retrieves. Set up to avoid time-consuming, frustrating tangles whenever you can.

4. For hunting over decoys select a shotgun with a more open choke. Set the spread so that the landing zone is in prime range for your gun. Restrict your shooting zone to a range at which you are confident you can cleanly kill the birds and mark that area with a stake, a confidence decoy or some other tangible, visible marker. It really adds challenge, excitement and a feeling of accomplishment to only take birds that are within your self-imposed range limits.

5. NAHC Member Mike Boeselager of Maribel, Wisconsin, finds it helpful to try something out of the ordinary when hunting geese that have seen a lot of hunting pressure in one locale. For example, few Wisconsin hunters use rag decoys, though everybody

hunts over fields full of shells. Mike has had good success scattering 50 dark goose rags in grassy fields within public hunting areas near his home. Though the birds usually don't actually work the spread, they often swing close to investigate and Mike gets his two-bird limit.

6. Utility companies frequently inspect the heavy rubber gauntlets used by their linemen. As a safety measure, the gloves are replaced at the first signs of wear or if there are holes. Many discarded gloves still are good enough to keep your hands dry while you retrieve floating decoys. They are generally large enough to slip right over your regular gloves.

7. If there is bare shoreline within the area you are hunting, be sure to put out some field-type decoys along the shore, as well as floaters in the water. Unless the birds of a flock are spooked, they are seldom in the water at one time. And in extremely shallow water, field decoys will sit more naturally than floaters.

8. In dry years, when runoff ponds are few and far between, consider creating your own portable pond. It sounds weird, but you can "make" a pond by using clear, heavy-duty plastic like the kind used as vapor barrier in house construction. This plastic comes in sheets large enough to create a realistic pond. Turn the edges under and weight it carefully so the material won't flutter. Place a few field decoys on the plastic and some around the edges. Placed in a stubble field on a regular flyway, this "pond" can be deadly, especially on migrant birds new to the area!

9. Don't let ice-up deter you from decoying ducks late in the season. If you're fortunate enough to find a small patch of open water, you'll probably only need a half a dozen decoys or less to create a convincing spread. If you can't find open water, try to create some by smashing the ice into large chunks and using a pusher pole to slide them back under the unbroken ice. But be careful, this is hard and dangerous work. Use a moving decoy rig of some kind to slow refreezing of your honeyhole.

10. Before picking a site to spread your decoys, look carefully for any obstacles that might deter the birds from decoying. Ducks may not want to fly near power lines, for example, and geese tend to avoid isolated patches of cover in open fields.

14

Hunting For Dangerous Game
by Hal Swiggett

Many animals can be dangerous under the right ... make that the wrong ... conditions. It doesn't have to be a leopard in Africa or a brown bear in Alaska. A wounded, cornered or sick animal of almost any species can pose all the danger any hunter would want to handle.

The secrets for dealing with dangerous game, if there are any, is to be constantly alert, carry enough gun for the job at hand and try to expect the unexpected. But sooner or later, regardless of how cautious you might be, you will be caught with your drawers at half mast. Stall that encounter as long as possible, but always be prepared for it.

Trouble seems to have a way of singling me out in particular. There's been more than one occasion on which I've seen a hunt suddenly turn dangerous.

Making The Bull Angry

Once, an old buffalo (American Bison) bull had wandered away one too many times. Once those cantankerous critters get the wanderlust there's no fence known to mankind that will keep them at home.

This bull was finally found a long way from home. The old boy's time had come. I was invited to the buffalo burger party, but was assigned the task to obtain the main course.

The hunt proceeded, but the gent who was tasked with actually shooting the bull botched the job. Two large caliber rifle bullets, neither in the right place, created a situation the hunter couldn't cope with. He hightailed it for safer parts.

I got the call even though all I had with me was my 4⅝-inch customized Ruger Super Blackhawk stuffed with five Remington 240-grain hollowpoints. (This was a very long time ago as can be ascertained from the loads I was shooting in those days.)

The bull was upset. In fact, he was angry. He was really in no danger of dying from either wound unless possibly from pneumonia brought on by wind blowing through his body. I hadn't caused his predicament, but he didn't know it.

We played footsie through the mesquite for a while. Then when he got tired of the game, the 2,000-pound bull squared off to flatten his 155-pound tormentor—namely, me.

Feeling secure and confident with both hands firmly wrapped around the Ruger, I brought the sights to bear between his eyes.

The hammer dropped.

The bull didn't.

That bullet glanced off his forehead as if it had hit a flat rock. Just like in a Western movie, it zinged away into yonder territory.

About then, the party livened up decidedly!

Eventually I was able to get a bullet into his left lung, then after a bit more toying with each other (he did most of the toying), one in his right lung. Shortly thereafter, he stood still so my last two shots were placed the same, one in each lung. Had I been using 320-grain bullets, which we have now, it would not have been necessary to puncture both sides.

Even more power was called for on another rogue animal hunt.

A Beisa Oryx, on a non-hunting exotic ranch in Texas, had killed a hired hand. Try as he might, the ranch biologist couldn't safely get close enough to tranquilize the bull, so I was called to do the job permanently.

Oryx are an African antelope that don't take well to domestication, and this particular animal had injured two people earlier and should have already been destroyed or at least dehorned before he had killed the ranch hand.

When we found the bull, a piece of the ranch hand's shirt was still hanging from one horn. This horn was broken three or so inches from the tip. Not off, but fractured like a tree limb bent to the breaking point. Both the horns and its face were covered in human blood.

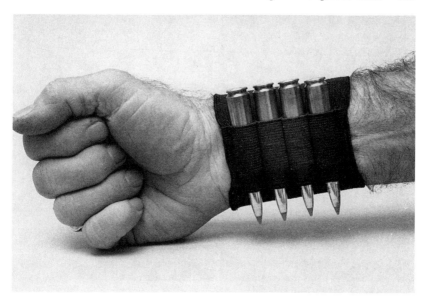

When using a pistol on dangerous game and a fast second shot is needed, a wrist band cartridge holder is recommended.

Despite all of our careful maneuvering, we could not get him out of thick brush for a clear shot. The terrain was such that there were strips of cleared ground amid the heavy cover.

Despite the biologist's extremely loud and pointed protests, I got out of the pickup.

The bull was no more than 30 yards inside the cover, but it was much too dense for a shot. We were only a few yards from the edge.

I walked slowly around in front of the vehicle. The animal's eyes were on my every move.

Crazed with a desire to anchor another human, the critter spun and headed for me. Anticipating what was going to happen, I had already leveled my .45-70 Gov. custom T/C chest high, at the corner of the brush. As the bull cleared the brushline, the big .45 bullet slammed into his chest.

No longer interested in discombobulating my anatomy, he plunged back into the thick stuff. We found him, down but not dead, two rows over. A neck shot finished the soiree.

The shoulder mount of that oryx hangs in the Handgun Hunters Museum and Hall of Fame in Mt. Clemens, Michigan. The museum is located in the Mag-na-port International building and is open to

Leaning against a tree or large rock provides good solid support, especially when using the powerful .47-70 single action. Many dangerous game have been taken from this position.

the public. It is well worth the visit if you are in the area. The museum boasts a wide variety of big game trophies, both dangerous and otherwise, all taken by handgun hunters.

Don't Take Chances

Sometimes danger is in the eye of the beholder, and the animal he is after.

My Colorado guide, Fran, and I were making our way toward a rather nice mule deer buck. It had been shot from across a canyon by another member of our party.

Hand signals guided us along the narrow trail about midway up the mountainside. Brush was not dense, but it prevented us from seeing around bends in the trail.

As we rounded a slight curve, Fran, who was in front hugging the left side so I could see past him, dived, with no warning, into the brush on his left. I duplicated his performance at the same instant, but to my right.

The buck was down, lengthwise in the trail, head toward us. We cautiously eased our way alongside to discover he was dead.

Fran looked at me. I looked back. We were in silent agreement. Both of us had seen the buck blink both eyes. With no more than 6 feet between Fran and the buck's nose, one place we didn't need to be was on a narrow mountain trail in front of that wounded deer. That eyelid movement must have been his final twitch, but it sure made for an exciting moment.

Nice Shot, But ...

The thermometer was hovering near 10 degrees. The watch on my left wrist confirmed the time as being 11:15 a.m., which meant this day wasn't going to get much warmer. About that same time a 6x6 bull elk strolled along a game trail considerably higher than where my guide and I stood. My rifle was a .375 H&H Magnum shooting carefully handloaded Hornady 270-grain bullets to factory velocity. It was sighted in at 2 inches high at 200 yards. The scope was a 6X Weaver. I was prepared for long range.

I knew, through practice, where the bullet printed at 300 and 400 yards. I estimated the distance to be 325 yards, held for the bullet to drop into the center of his lungs and squeezed the trigger.

My intention was for the bull to come down the mountain as he died from the bullet wound in his lungs. Instead he took maybe 20 steps ahead, stayed on his trail and collapsed. Dead. Dead, dead.

I had underestimated the distance and made a perfect heart shot, a shot my guide praised and later talked to all who would listen about it.

Now, to my way of thinking, no hunter in his right mind would try a heart shot at that distance, 400-plus yards. The difference between a heart shot and a complete miss or broken leg, depending on the angle, is only a few inches.

My guide, although praising the shot, said, "You're supposed to shoot them so they take themselves down the mountain before they die." He reminded me of this several times over the next half-dozen hours as we worked the field-dressed bull down to where he could get his 4-wheel-drive pickup close enough to attach the truck winch to it and drag it out.

Where's the danger you ask? Ever try to live up to the reputation you get from a big-mouthed guide who tells every stranger in the street about his client's 400-yard heart shot? It ain't easy!

Same Song, Second Verse

The coyote had responded to my call. He came straight in so fast his feet barely touched the ground. About 100 yards out he caught in mid-stride that all wasn't as it should be. He did a full

180-degree turn, still in the air, and departed the same way he had come. Same speed, opposite direction.

What appeared to be way out yonder he stopped, turned around, looked back at my coyote hunting partner and me and sat down on his haunches. He pointed his nose skyward and barked, telling one and all within hearing distance that two jerks were sitting under that little mesquite and meant him no good.

Turning to my partner, I said, "I simply have to wish that rascal well." As I spoke my wrists snuggled down against my knees, my back was braced against the mesquite, and the .44 Magnum Super Blackhawk sought him out.

He was so far away I put the entire front-sight blade up, then actually placed him as though sitting on the blade. When the hammer dropped, his nose was still pointed toward the sky, but I knew the shot was good. I don't know how, but I knew that bullet would find its target.

A moment later that coyote dropped like it had been hit on the head with a hammer. My partner said, "I wish I hadn't seen that." While still seated and waiting for what had happened to soak in, I asked why. He quickly responded with, "Nobody is going to believe it."

My partner stepped it off. A tall man, he paced off 307 steps. Like I said, this guy was tall and had a habit of stretching his steps, so I know it was at least 307 yards. Possibly a bit farther. The 240-grain bullet had dropped in over one eye. No way it could have been done on purpose. I've often said if I ever have to choose between being good or lucky I'll take luck every time.

15

Ins And Outs Of Handloading
by Bob Hagel

Where is no doubt that more shooters are reloading their own
ammunition than ever before. It also seems to be a safe bet
that the percentage of shooters who make up their own ammunition
is higher today than during any period since the advent of self-
contained cartridges. During the muzzleloading era everyone was a
handloader, of necessity. The early cartridge arms were rimfires,
or used other ignition systems which are no longer in use, and few
were reloadable—which was one of the major criticisms of
cartridge guns. The advent of the Berdan and, particularly, the Boxer
centerfire ignition systems with replaceable primers inaugurated
the modern era and revived the practice of loading one's own
ammunition.

Handloading Boxer-primed centerfire cartridges was a simple
matter in the black powder era, factories and individual shooters
alike simply filled the case with powder. Not until smokeless
powder came into use during the last years of the 19th century did
precise charges become critical to safety. However, despite the
safety and simplicity of black powder cartridge reloading, and
despite the availability of reloading tools from the gun-makers, the
great majority of frontiersmen—hunters, trappers, cowboys, ranchers,
miners and prospectors—used mostly factory ammunition. A notable
exception because of the large amounts of ammunition used was
the professional buffalo hunter, who reloaded his cases each

evening, or in the case of a large party of hunters, some member did it nearly full-time. But because of the legends of the handloading buffalo hunters, it is assumed that handloading was common on the western frontier. Not so.

When I was growing up in the West, I knew many old frontiersmen who had spent a lifetime with a rifle in hand or hung on the side of the horse, and very few of them had ever loaded a single round of ammunition. My father was a good example of a slightly later period when the single shot had given way to the repeater during the late 1890s and the early part of this century. Dad hunted constantly from the time he arrived in the then-new state of Idaho, but he had never loaded a round of ammunition until I started stuffing my own in the early '30s. In fact, the first man I ever knew who did a great deal of handloading was Elmer Keith, and it was my early association with Elmer that started my handloading career.

Back in those early days of handloading, the reloading tools were very simple, usually consisting of a bullet mold and a tong-type loading tool. There were variations of these tools, but all that I am familiar with had a minimum of parts. Some had only one other part besides the loading chamber, and that was a decapping punch that was either inserted in the loading chamber or used separately by inserting over a hole in a block of wood or metal, and tapping the punch. There was usually a separate opening, hole or slot in the tong body where the unprimed case was inserted for seating a new primer, and a primer seating stem shaped to fit the primer pushed the new cap home when the tool handles were closed.

I have an old Winchester reloading tool for the .45 Government (.45-70) cartridge with a patent date of Feb. 14, 1894, that is simplicity to the *n*th degree. Except for decapping and charging, all reloading operations are performed with the tong handles and a single-piece loading chamber. The case is reprimed by inserting it into a rounded notch in the tool forward of the hinge pin, but sizing, bullet seating and crimping are done in one operation in the loading chamber. The loading chamber screws into the handle with very coarse threads, and has an inside diameter small enough to size the case to fit the chamber. The primed, charged case, with the bullet inserted into its mouth, is started into the chamber which is then screwed down tight with the handles open. This sizes the case down while seating the bullet nearly all the way. When the handle is closed the case is forced down just the right amount to crimp in

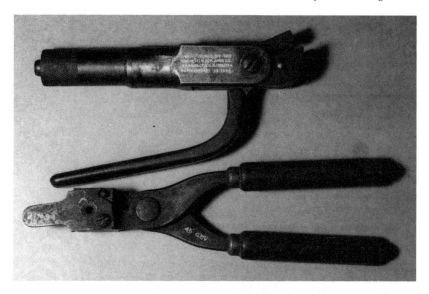

This Winchester bullet mold and tong-type reloading tool for the .45-70 cartridge is the ultimate in simplicity. The loading chamber (top) handles partial case resizing, bullet seating and crimping in a single operation. The patent date is Feb. 14, 1894.

the crimping groove of the bullet formed by the mold furnished with the reloading tool. I don't know how well it would work when reloading for more than one rifle and using the same cases, but it works well for one rifle considering the pressures the cartridge developed in loads of that day.

My first reloading tool was a Lyman No. 3 (for rimmed cases) tong tool that I used for the .30-40 cartridge, but which would work equally well for the .35 and .405 Winchester cartridges with different caliber accessories. It also produced good reloads with the .44 S&W Special cartridge component parts. Of course, these tong tools did not have the power to full-length resize rifle cases; if you wanted to do that you had to use a separate drive-in type resize die. This was of little consequence to me at the time because pressures had to be held down in the old Krag rifle anyway.

These small, simple tools turned out reasonably good ammunition for most practical purposes and were certainly simple to use and economical to buy, and the same thing can be said for the modern tools like the Lee and Pak-Tool. There is little doubt that this type of reasonably priced reloading tool has started a lot of reloaders who otherwise probably would never have started reloading at all. Neither is there any doubt that it is possible to turn out accurate and

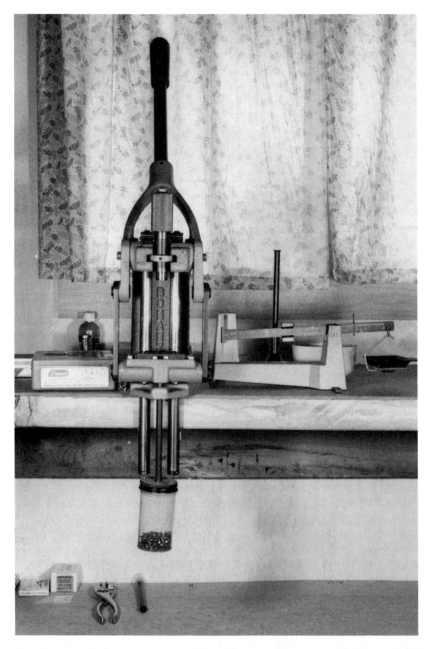

The Bonanza Co-Ax press is one of the most versatile ever made. The modified C-frame has a minimum spring and the linkage hookup is powerful. It also has a positive primer catcher and very rapid-change die arrangement.

reliable ammunition with them, but I am not completely convinced that they are the tools that are the best choice for all beginning reloaders. If the beginning reloader is reasonably certain that he will load for only one or two cartridges, and that those cartridges will always be loaded to mild pressures, then they are a good choice. On the other hand, if he has (or intends to buy) several rifles and/or pistols, and if he wants to realize the full potential of any or all of those cartridges, then I think he is better off starting his reloading career with a good, but reasonably-priced (of course), reloading press.

The main problem encountered in using one of the small hand-held reloading tools is that they will not full-length resize rifle cartridge cases. If a case is to be fired very many times at the pressures used in most modern rifle cartridges, even when staying well within factory pressure specs, it will have to be full-length resized periodically. And if you intend to realize the full potential of the cartridge in your rifle, you will have to work up a load to the top pressure level that the rifle and case will handle safely, then back it off to where it makes an accurate, safe, trouble-free load under all of the conditions where it will be used. To do this you will have to full-length resize the cases in working up the load, and with many cartridges they will have to be resized full-length every time they are fired. Also, if the reloader intends to do any case forming, such as making a case for which brass is in short supply from one that is easy to obtain, or wildcatting by changing case body or shoulder, a powerful-leverage press is a necessity.

Considering all of this, and the fact that most shooters who take up handloading have more than one rifle or pistol to load for, and that they will almost certainly become addicted to reloading their own ammunition, it seems that the majority should have serious thoughts about buying a good press to start with.

There are many good presses on the market, and the most expensive are not necessarily the best. The first press I ever owned was an old Pacific Super, and I still use that press today after loading uncounted thousands of rounds of all sizes with it. That press is of the C-type, which simply means that the upper portion is shaped like the letter C. There are also O-types which have a circle of steel for better die support, and H-types which consist of a pair of vertical columns between which a movable die carrier rides. Variations of these basic press designs include turret heads holding all the dies necessary to load a cartridge, or several cartridges, by simply rotating the turret. Although there are numerous variations of all these types, each type is basically the same in principle, with the possible exception of the Bonanza Co-Ax, which is a unique combination of C and H features. The greatest difference within each type is the linkage setup which controls the power the press is capable of exerting.

Any of these frame types may have the same basic linkage design, but the type of frame dictates to a great extent how useful it is for heavy work. The less spring there is in the press frame the better that press is adapted to precision heavy-duty work. The principle of design indicates that the turret head press has more room for play and spring than the other two types, and is not as well suited to heavy forming jobs. It is, however, well adapted to speedy reloading of several calibers, and will turn out excellent ammunition with either neck or full-length resizing of the cases. *(Author's note: Some of the new turret presses developed since this was written are as rigid and free from spring as single-stage presses.)*

The C-type press varies somewhat in the amount of spring the frame has under heavy pressure, which depends a great deal on the design and depth of the throat of the C, but there is some spring with any of them under very heavy loads. They are certainly ample for any resizing job, and I have formed large numbers of cases from heavy belted brass with the old Pacific Super.

But for the fellow who thinks that at some time he may want to do a lot of heavy case forming, and perhaps some bullet swaging on his loading press, the O press with the most powerful leverage hookups is ideal. These presses do all the other reloading chores just as well as the others, while having the power and lack of spring in the frame to do the toughest jobs with greater ease of operation.

When one becomes deeply involved in reloading where a great deal of test work is being done, a pair of presses side-by-side on the loading bench is a great convenience and time-saver. On my own bench in the reloading room I have the old Pacific Super set up beside an RCBS Rock Chucker. In normal loading the resizing die is in the RCBS with its O-frame and powerful linkage, and the seating die in the C-type Pacific. Primers are also seated in the Pacific in a separate operation. I like it better to prime with because I can feel the primer seat. This eliminates a separate priming tool and does an equally good job. All heavy case forming is done in the RCBS press because of its greater strength and minimum frame spring.

The old Pacific Super C reloading press (left) and the RCBS Rock Chucker press (right) make an ideal combination for rapid reloading of all sizes and styles of rifle cartridges. The O press with its powerful linkage and leverage is used for case resizing and forming; the C press for priming and bullet seating. While either press will do all reloading jobs, the pair set up this way simplifies and speeds test work.

For the advanced reloader who reloads several cartridges in quantity, both a powder measure and scale are needed. The scale is a "must" item, the measure is not. Also, the powder trickler and funnel with drip tube are very handy items.

On the loading bench in the chronograph room of my shop where many loads are tested simultaneously for accuracy and velocity, I use a Bonanza Co-Ax press, which is probably one of the most versatile presses ever made. It has a minimum of spring in its modified O-type frame, powerful linkage and leverage, and dies can be changed in a split second. If properly adjusted the priming arrangement is excellent, and the primer can be seated to match the depth of any pocket. As far as I know, it also provides the only sure-catch depriming arrangement.

Speaking of primers brings up whether a separate priming tool is a necessity for precision priming, or even a very desirable piece of bench equipment. These tools do a good job of priming but are far from a necessity. The main reason for using them is so you can feel the primer seat solidly against the bottom of the primer pocket. At least that is the way they should be used. It has been stated that their main function is to seat each primer to exactly the same depth. The main thing to remember in seating a primer is that for best results it should be seated all the way to the bottom of the pocket so that the anvil legs rest solidly. If it does not seat solidly it will be driven down by the impact of the firing pin, which may cause erratic ignition. You also have to consider that it must not protrude above the surface of the cartridge head. If it does, that case will be hard to chamber if it is headspaced correctly. In most cases made today it will take considerable pressure to seat the primer below the surface, and it is far better to exert a little extra pressure in seating a primer in a loading press, than not enough with a less powerful ''soft feel'' priming tool.

My experience in priming indicates that it is largely a matter of preference as to whether primers are seated with the loading press or in a separate priming tool. If the press you use will seat a primer so that you can feel it seat on the bottom of the pocket, then there is no reason you should not use it. If you can't be certain when it is bottoming without crushing the priming compound, then perhaps a separate priming tool is indicated. Be sure to clean primer pockets before seating the new primer because the residue often keeps the primer from seating deep enough so it is below the surface of the case head.

If the handloader intends to reload the same case many times, and especially if that case is full-length resized and is a high velocity number that develops high pressures, a case trimmer is about a must. There are many makes of trimmers, but basically nearly all are of two designs. One kind is used in a loading press; the case is inserted as in the resizing operation and the over-length neck protrudes above the top of the hardened trimmer die. The end of the neck is then simply filed flush with the top of the die. The other type is the lathe design where a cutting head trims the neck to the desired length by turning the trimmer handle by hand.

The die-type trimmer works very well, and is incorporated with the die made for forming cases, or as a single use unit, but it has two disadvantages: First, it is rather slow to use, and second, a die is required for each cartridge. While the trimmer die costs about one-third as much as the lathe type trimmer, the cost will be much higher if several different cartridges will be loaded. Also, there is no way to vary the length to which the neck will be trimmed— something that may prove desirable with certain types of chambers.

The lathe-type trimmer is fully adjustable for trim length, and most will accept cases with a length running from the .222 to the long Magnums like the .375 H&H. A single collet will also accept head diameters in the same range. Few will accept cases in the class of the big-rimmed cartridges like the .45-70 or .378-.460 Weatherby unless a separate collet is obtained, which is not always available. All that normally must be purchased for trimming different cartridges is a case neck pilot of the correct diameter; a single pilot of any given diameter will fit all cases which utilize that bullet diameter.

Some trimmers of this type are made to trim only. Others, Redding being an example, have a cutter blade that not only trims the neck but chamfers (bevels) it inside and out in the same operation. This system is very fast because it eliminates chamfering the case mouth in a separate operation; however, because the blade cuts from one side of the neck to adjust for all calibers, it is inclined to grab and chatter if a little too much pressure is exerted. The double-edge cutting head, as found on trimmers like the Forster, makes a little smoother and faster cut. In fact, the Forster trimmer is an extremely versatile tool because it may also be set up to precision-turn the case neck to any desired thickness by using optional neck turning accessories. (There may also be other trimmers with the same arrangement.) If the reloader intends to do much reloading of match grade ammunition, or ever expects to do any case forming where large cases are necked down a great deal, or perhaps the shoulder set back to form the new neck, he is well advised to buy a trimmer that is capable of outside neck turning. I prefer outside turning to inside reaming for most precision work. Once again, this is my personal opinion.

There is some disagreement among reloaders as to whether the powder charge should be weighed or measured for the best results. Some reloaders contend that bulk is a more accurate form of measurement than weight because there is a possibility that the powder may vary in moisture content, which will affect bulk less than weight. My personal view is that this is splitting hairs pretty fine, and that it has little bearing on an accurate, uniform charge. What is more important is that the powder measure be capable of throwing consistent charges. And if not, will the charges be close enough for the kind of shooting being done? The proponents of metered charges have a ready answer for that by pointing out that bench rest shooters usually measure the charges they use, and none of us need be told what kind of accuracy those loads deliver. However, those measures are known to throw a given powder accurately, or the measures are modified so they will. But it really isn't all that simple for the reloader looking at tools of the trade for

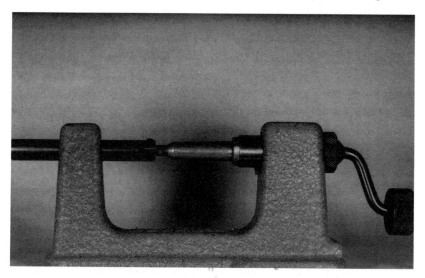

A case trimmer of some kind is essential to reload for cartridges that develop high pressures, or any case that will be reloaded several times. This Redding trimmer has a head that chamfers the case mouth while trimming, thereby eliminating a separate chamfering operation.

the use he will have for them, and what he wishes to spend for equipment.

The simplest form of measuring powder is, of course, the dipper measure that holds a certain amount of powder (for a specified powder) and is dipped into the powder and leveled off with a straight edge. While reasonably reliable loads can be made up with this method using powders that are not too touchy to load, and that develop mild pressures, it is, at best, pretty crude. If you have doubts about that statement, try weighing a few dipper charges. For better results, hold the dipper over a cup of powder, and fill it to overflowing with another dipper, then strike off the surplus.

As far as the drum-type powder measures go, they all work on about the same principle where a stroke of the handle fills a chamber that is readily adjustable for any desired charge likely to be used. Some have separate metering chambers for loading rifle and pistol cartridges, the pistol chamber having less powder capacity to afford a higher degree of accuracy, at least in theory. One thing they all have in common is that if a fine-grained powder is used, the charges are quite uniform, the spherical powders usually metering the best. As powder granules become larger, and

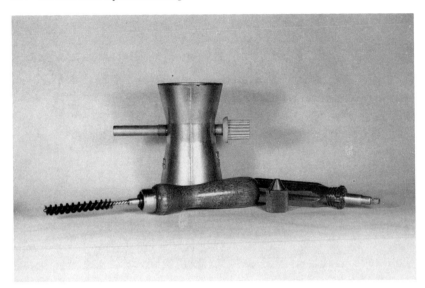

These small inexpensive tools—neck cleaning brush, inside-outside neck chamfering tool, primer pocket cleaner and powder trickler—are highly desirable items on any loading bench, but they are not essential for making quality reloads.

especially with extruded "log type" powders, uniformity of charges goes down. And, of course, the larger the charge the more room for error. This is one good reason why measuring bench rest charges works well. With any measure I have ever used, there will be a variation between charges of coarse-grained powders like IMR-4350 and H-4831 of as much as one grain with heavy charges in magnum capacity cases. This is also about average for factory loaded ammunition with similar powders in the same cases, so if you wish to improve on the uniformity found in factory loads, there is some food for thought here.

I seldom use a powder measure in my work because when testing and/or developing loads, the charge is continually changing —weighing charges can be accomplished in less time than it takes to get a measure adjusted correctly for the charge wanted. However, once a pistol load with the fine-grained powders and small charges is developed, the measure is used with charges thrown directly into the case for quantity loading. The same procedure is followed with small capacity rifle cases with dense powders, but when loading large capacity rifle cases with coarse-grained extruded powders, even in quantity, the measure is adjusted to throw an average charge about .5 grain below that wanted, dropped into the scale pan and then brought up to exact weight with a dipper or trickler. A powder trickler is very handy here because the charge can be brought up to weight without going over once you learn how to use it efficiently.

If you plan to load quite a few different cartridges and powders, a continuous-screw drum adjustment, marked with micrometer-type or other repeatable settings, can be a considerable time-saver. Not only can you record the setting for a particular charge, making it easy to repeat at a later date, you can also determine the approximate setting for a particular powder charge by setting the measure to throw a light and a heavy charge, then plotting the charges thrown for these settings on graph paper and drawing a straight line between the points. By referring to the graph, the approximate charge setting for that powder can be determined; it won't be exactly right with most measures, but it should be close.

As to whether the beginning reloader should buy a powder scale or a measure, or both, let's look at it this way: You can get along very well for any kind of reloading with a good scale, but a measure is unsatisfactory for some aspects of reloading, and of no value whatsoever for load development work. Also, a scale must be used to set the measure. If you do a lot of reloading in quantity for the same load, load a lot of small capacity rifle cases with fine grain powders, or pistol ammunition, a good powder measure will see continuous use. It should be remembered, however, that it is not a necessity for the beginner and will cost approximately as much as the powder scale, thereby doubling the cost of the powder charging equipment.

Which brand of powder scale the beginning reloader buys is largely a matter of choice. Most of them are accurate to at least .1 grain. If various brands are compared at different powder charge readings, it may be found that there is a slight variation, as much as .2 grain, or more in some instances, when weighing some of the heavier charges. This is of little actual concern because it isn't enough to upset a load in any way, and the charge will always be the same when weighed on the same scale. There is no reason whatsoever to buy the most expensive powder scale for any kind of reloading. The one consideration above all others is that the scale should have a magnetic damping arrangement to settle the pointer quickly. Some of the cheapest scales do not have this feature, but it greatly speeds up the charging process while saving a lot of wear and tear on the reloader's nerves.

Although magnetically damped handloading scales have been

on the market for almost two decades, some experienced handloaders still don't understand how they work, and contend that the "pull of the magnets can cause false readings." Not so. The damper vane attached to the beam is non-magnetic, so it cannot be attracted by the magnets; however, it is an electrical conductor—usually copper. When the vane swings between the magnets, a minute electric current is produced which creates a magnetic field around the vane; the faster the swing, the greater the current and the stronger the magnetic field. This induced magnetic field alternately is attracted or repelled by the magnets in the scale base, damping (slowing) the swing of the beam, but when the beam stops swinging after a couple of cycles, the lack of motion results in the disappearance of the electrical field so the vane is no longer affected by the magnets.

There are countless items made for use on the reloading bench—ranging from useful to plain gadgetry—that are made for no other reason except that the gadget-happy American is sure to buy them if they get the right kind of advertising exposure. They also include small useful tools like primer pocket cleaners and case mouth chamfering tools, powder tricklers and case length gauges that are certainly helpful but not "must" items. There are such exotic pieces of mechanism as case tumblers and polishers, and dial reading powder scales. But the tools that have been suggested are the ones the average reloader will need, or at least should consider if he intends to get serious about reloading his own ammunition.

16

Clothing And Other Gear

by Michael Lapinski

When hunting in the West, September can be unusually balmy, with temperatures quite warm at midday and cool in the mornings. However, a storm front can rapidly move in and bring with it rain or snow. The hunter should prepare to wear mostly warm-weather clothes; however, he should also bring proper clothing for rain or snow conditions.

In September, bowhunters usually wear long sleeve shirts with camouflaged clothing over it during fair weather. This will keep a hunter warm during the brisk early morning hours, but not overheat him in the afternoon.

A weather front bringing rain in September will also bring cooler temperatures. A good set of rainpants and a jacket are necessities for any hunter, because it could rain every day for a week. (In fact, it is vital that a bowhunter is hunting in his rain gear in wet weather. I've killed five of my 10 bow-killed elk when it was raining.)

An early-season snowstorm in September is a common occurrence in the West. The snow usually melts within a few days, and the weather returns to normal. A hunter should bring a set of wool clothes so he can take advantage of the good hunting following a snowstorm. A light wool shirt and wool pants allow a hunter to comfortably move in the snow.

Footwear should include a pair of light leather boots for fair weather, uninsulated rubber boots for wet weather and insulated rubber boots for snow. Many bowhunters wear tennis shoes for silent movement through the forest when the weather is rather warm and dry.

The Early Rifle Season (October)

Expect cold weather in October. Snow usually does not cover the ground at the beginning of October, but by the end of the month, snow is common. The early-October hunter should bring a set of wool clothes, including a wool shirt, pants and longjohns and a wool jacket; he should also bring a set of light cotton hunting clothes, so he can interchange his hunting outfit depending upon the weather. If the temperature is 20 degrees but clear, he can skip the heavy wool pants and wear longjohns and cotton pants.

Later in the month when snow is on the ground, wear wool. Those heavy wool pants will keep you warm, and they will shed the snow without absorbing moisture. A goose down vest is acceptable during cold weather, but avoid other goose down garments when snow hunting because down loses its insulating quality when it gets wet.

A bowhunter in October has a problem. Temperatures below freezing are common, and a bowhunter must keep warm, yet remain camouflaged. A bowhunter can dress adequately by wearing camouflage that is a size larger than normal. That way, he can wear longjohns and an extra wool shirt underneath his camo clothes without restricting movement or circulation.

Footgear should include insulated leather boots for cold or dry hunting conditions and insulated rubber boots for hunting in the wet snow.

The Late Season (November)

Expect deep snow and cold temperatures in November. Wool clothes should be worn, and that includes longjohns, socks, pants, shirt and coat. A hunter can spend all day moving through snow covered brush and tree limbs, but stay warm and dry with wool.

The late-season hunter often is in a quandary to wear the proper clothes during a day's hunt. Bitter cold, below-zero temperatures are not uncommon in the mountains, and the cold quickly seeps through a hunter who is wearing a wool jacket if he is standing still for hours watching an open area. But if he wears extra clothing, he will perspire too much when he begins to struggle through the snow. That's where a goose down vest is valuable. A hunter can wear the vest while he is on his stand, and then put it in his pack when he begins moving.

Footgear should include a good pair of insulated rubber boots for hunting. Bring along a pair of leather insulated boots for wearing around camp.

Survival Gear

No matter where or when you're hunting, you will need to have survival gear. It is very common for hunters to carry a day pack and a survival kit. Some hunters prefer to carry the survival kit within the pack; however, it is recommended to carry them separately. That way, if a hunter is separated from his pack for any reason, he will still have his survival kit.

Before venturing out on a planned hunting trip, be sure you are aware of various signaling techniques and survival and first-aid methods. Also, it is extremely important to know how to use your compass and topographical map.

Day Pack Items

When taking a vacation, the common rule is to pack "light." This also applies for a hunting trip. The less cumbersome, the better. When hunting various species of game, a day pack's items may vary. The following list of items, however, is fairly universal. But feel free to add to it according to your situation.

● The pack should be made of sturdy, waterproof material with padded shoulder straps. The color is usually blaze orange or camouflage.

● An extra pair of wool socks can come in mighty handy, especially if hunting during rain.

● Shooting gloves can be a big asset, especially when weather tends to be cold.

● Drag rope is important when deer hunting. It can also help you pull items up to your tree stand.

● A topographical map is a must when hunting any type of terrain.

● A pocket knife is essential.

● A knife sharpening stone should also be included.

● You never know when foul weather will appear, so a rainsuit is important.

● A canteen for drinking and cooking is needed, as well dehydrated high-energy foods.

● Some hunters like to take their gun cleaning set.

Day-pack items include, but are not limited to: pack, extra wool socks, extra shooting gloves, drag rope, topo map, pocket knife, knife-sharpening stone, rain suit, canteen, high-energy foods (such as hot cocoa mix), gun cleaning set, toilet paper, compass, survival guide, waterproof matches, extra ammunition, smoke signal, flashlight, binoculars, flagging tape, police whistle, lip protection, first-aid kit and camera.

● Toilet paper is also important for many different reasons. It can help with trailing, as well as "other" duties.

● A compass should be included within the day pack or somewhere on your body.

● A small, pocket-sized survival guide can be very helpful in case of emergencies.

● You should always have a packet of waterproof matches.

● Extra ammunition serves its purpose on many, many trips.

● A signaling kit (smoke signal) should be included.

● When caught in the dark, a flashlight is a must.

● Some type of flagging tape should be carried.

● A police whistle can be used for signaling or alerting danger.

● Lip ointment helps prevent chapping from the sun or wind.

● A small first-aid kit should be packed for minor injuries.

● And a small or disposable camera is great to have for those memorable shots.

Remember that this is just a basic list and may vary from hunter to hunter and trip to trip.

Survival Kit Items

The importance of a survival kit cannot be stressed enough. Any hunter that has been in an uneasy and frightening situation should know the advantage of being prepared. It would be nice to never have such an experience, but it can happen. The following list of items is not a comprehensive list and can vary.

● The kit carrier should be compact and easy to carry. A common carrier is an Army surplus first-aid pouch.

● A backup topographical map should be included, in case you are separated from your day pack.

● A compact space blanket is a must.

● Sterile pads for wrapping wounds helps prevent infection.

● High-energy foods should always be included.

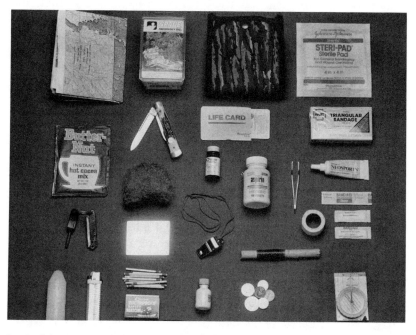

Survival kit items include, but are not limited to: topo map, space blanket, Army surplus first-aid pouch, sterile pads, high-energy foods (such as hot cocoa), pocket knife, survival guide, triangular bandages, steel wool, water purification tablets, aspirin, tweezers, antibiotic ointment, adhesive bandages, white tape, metal match, signal mirror, police whistle, fishing line, candle, lighter, waterproof matches, wire saw, small tackle box, coins and backup compass.

- A backup pocket knife is essential.
- Once again a pocket-sized survival guide is a necessity.
- Triangular bandages help with patching wounds.
- Steel wool can help with starting tinder fires.
- Water purification tablets should always be carried.
- Aspirin will help relieve pain if needed.
- Tweezers come in handy for several different reasons.
- Antibiotic ointment helps speed the healing process for minor scratches, burns or abrasions, and prevents infection.
- White adhesive tape helps wrap wounds.
- A metal match is advantageous.
- A signal mirror, police whistle and signaling kit are important when in need of assistance.
- Also a candle and lighter can help in signaling.
- Waterproof matches should be included in your survival kit, as well as your day pack.
- Fishing line can be used for various reasons, including fishing.
- A small tackle box can be created for use.
- Some type of wire saw should be carried for emergency situations. It comes in handy for cutting wood, etc. for shelter.
- Always make sure you have coins for emergency situations, especially for using a telephone.
- And a backup compass should always be carried in your kit.

Once again, this list can be added to or subtracted from, depending upon the individual hunter's needs. However, be aware that something can go wrong in any hunting situation.

Topographical Maps

Topographical maps were covered somewhat in Chapter 8. Learning to use them can be quite frustrating; it takes time and hands-on experience in order to become comfortable with them. It is very important to know the terrain you are going to hunt "before" hunting it. A good hunter is always prepared, and "topo" maps are the first step. The U.S. Geological Survey provides state maps which can be ordered. Also remember that topo maps act as a "base" for research. You should never rely solely on just a map. (As you know, change happens constantly and maps need to be revised.)

After receiving the map of the terrain you plan to hunt, it is best to thoroughly study it before venturing out on your quest. You can bring your hunting partners together at camp to study it before

A topographical map shows various features in detail. These features include natural things such as small lakes, rivers and streams, marshland and steep ridges. It will also show man-made features which include houses, roads, trails and railroad grade.

Topographical maps can be invaluable aids for all types of hunting, whether you use a muzzleloader, rifle or bow. These bowhunters are examining a map together.

the hunt. Also, it is important to take it with you and mark features on it that are not already indicated. Another important step to take before actually hunting is scouting. Using your topo map and a good set of binoculars, glass the area for specific habitat and fresh sign of the game you plan to hunt. An example of this would be locating deer beds or droppings and marking them on your map. This helps you understand patterns and specific habitat that animals prefer. A good topo map is essential for all hunters, whether they are bowhunters, muzzleloaders or riflemen.

Special Gear For Self-Guided Hunts

The hunter who makes a self-guided hunt must be sure that his equipment is adequate. Time spent correcting inadequacies in equipment choice and quality will mean less hunting time. Basically, a hunter should bring enough equipment to provide food, warmth and shelter.

Shelter is important. If you can't keep out the elements, your

When scouting with topo maps before deer season, add deer-sign locations to your map. If you locate a deer bed, mark it down. Even though deer usually will not bed in the same exact spot for long, they will bed in the near vicinity.

dream trip will be a miserable experience. A camper trailer or motor home works fine. Otherwise, a tent must be used.

Hunters make the mistake of bringing one tent to live in for two weeks under various weather conditions. Rain and snow make clothes wet, and with one tent there is nowhere to dry them. And the cooking chore that was planned for outside is a real ordeal if the weather turns nasty. Smart hunters bring along two sturdy tents: one for sleeping, the other for cooking and hanging wet clothes.

You will need a heat source for cooking. A small sheet metal wood stove is one option; however, finding dry wood is often a problem. A kerosene heater is a good alternative. It will keep the tent warm and clothes dry, and it can burn while you're hunting. Don't expect to heat your cook tent with the cook stove. It does not put out enough heat to keep the tent warm, and it will be impossible to dry out damp clothing.

Bathing Facilities

The early-season hunter can purchase a commercial shower bag filled with water and heated by the sun, or he can simply rig up a primitive shower using a pail hung from a tree with some holes poked into its bottom.

A shower is impossible in November with deep snow and cold temperatures. A hunter will have to take a sponge bath. Water is heated and poured into a low, wide tub; the person crouches down and washes with a sponge. This can be done in a corner of the warm cook tent without much discomfort to the bather.

Sleeping Bags
A good sleeping bag is essential. A bag with a minimum 5 pounds fill (about a minus-10 degree rating) will be needed even in the early-season. It may reach 80 degrees at midday in September, but fall nights in the mountains are brisk. Place a thick sponge pad under the sleeping bag to make it soft. Also a plastic ground cloth helps prevent moisture from seeping into your bed!

General Camping Equipment
The following list of basic camping equipment is for three hunters taking a self-guided trip. You may need to add to it depending upon your situation and number of hunters.
- Two tents (10x10)
- A Coleman cook stove
- Three sets of eating utensils
- A portable table and chairs
- Two gas lanterns
- A heating stove
- A large basin for sponge bath
- Three sleeping bags (5-pound fill)
- Three sponge pads
- A set of cooking utensils
- Tarp to cover game, etc.
- A 5-gallon water jug
- A shovel for latrine purposes
- A large basin for dishes

The excitement of a hunting trip can be overwhelming and difficult to equal. However, do not let it interfere with your preparation for safety and comfort. Research and thorough planning are more valuable than most hunters realize.

Index